# I Wish Death Would Take A Vacation

## My Story

## (A Mini Memoir)

# I Wish Death Would Take A Vacation

## My Story

## (A Mini Memoir)

Joy M. Mills

For ye may all prophesy one by one,
that all may learn, and all may be comforted.

~1 Corinthians 14:31 ~

Library of Congress Number: 2017917939
ISBN-13: 978-0-9854367-1-1
ISBN-10: 0-9854367-1-9



The names of some individuals have been changed. Such names are indicated by an asterisk (*) the first time each appears in the narrative.



This book was printed in the United States of America.

Published by Lightsource Publications

This book is not intended to provide and does not constitute medical, legal or other professional advice. This book was written to support, not replace medical or psychiatric treatment. Please seek professional care if you feel you have a condition.

## WHERE MIDNIGHT RUNS

By Joy M. Mills

Beyond the stars - Where Midnight Runs…
Our life here done
Sunshine begins!
How can we grieve?
Why is it so?
We are human
Everyone must go…

The sad part is
No one really knows.
Some of us young
With so much life and potential it seems.
If only we all could spend
Our time here and give
The love
The hope
Encourage each other
Because our time is short
From the first breath we take
Until the last one is done.
We will go beyond - Where Midnight Runs…

This isn't negative
It isn't really death
It's life renewing
In a different form.
The rest of us weep
When our loved ones are gone.
The pain
The tears
We all feel and shed.
We take it so for granted
Life I mean
We don't stop to think about dead.

An awful word
It doesn't make sense
To those left behind.
We can't jump the fence.
They are not faraway
They are forever near
Our angels
Our help
Is what they have become
Beyond the sky - Where Midnight Runs....

They are at peace and so must we be.
Their bodies are gone
Their spirits set free.
"Remember the promise"
Again we will see them
Hold them close
So grieve not my friends.
Easily said
Your loved one
Has risen
Their soul is alive
No such word as gone
Beyond the sky - Where Midnight Runs…

So laughter through tears
When your heart aches so bad
Remember their smiles and try not to be sad.
They have gone beyond
The Stars
To a better place
No more heartache
No more pain
Where Midnight Runs…

# Dedication

For Mom:

I realized everyone you know will not be around forever which should enrich and deepen our love and relationships. Life is not a movie; you need to have a plan. Have an artist's ambition but an engineer's mindset. Thank you Mom. I found my voice.

To those who might judge me:

Thank you,
For without adversity,
I would not have reached my full potential
and found my way.

~J.M.

# Contents

# Introduction

This book was put off, postponed and then my mother died. It took her death to get me here. I found myself pitching this book. I had no idea what I was doing at the time but knew it had to be three books. After all, I did not want to write War and Peace. I knew I had to give my mother a voice. One she was never allowed in her lifetime. It could not be white-washed for her sake and my own.

There were three titles thrown out there over a couple of years. Then I remembered a dream I had two years ago. In that dream, someone was telling me after reading the final edits to my book it should be titled "When Death Takes A Vacation." It was a very strange dream. I woke up thinking, "Why would I write a book like that much less give it that title?" I began thinking about what that meant. There was no doubt I was ready for death to take a vacation as many others were experiencing the same thing and learning how to deal with grief or having to let go.

A focus group was given four titles and a brief synopsis for evaluation. It came back a resounding, across the board, educated, 18 to 70 plus-year-olds, they would pick up and read, "I Wish Death Would Take A Vacation - My Story." They found it to be intriguing and could not wait for the finished book. It has been a painful project.

Here is the thing - Why Me - is a weakening phrase. It only serves to increase our feeling of victimhood. It makes us feel incapable of dealing with the situations at hand. When we think about what is next, we gain back control and can figure out what to do. Sometimes in doing nothing, everything gets done.

Life is short, and we are human. These past fifteen months I have been marooned in a well of grief, at times feeling very alone surrounded by people. It is a place where I am unable to articulate the wound that clutches at my soul. My attention oscillates with an assault of questions and an endless loop of uncertainty. There are so many others that are grieving following shock and the pain of the death of those close to them, young and old alike. Eventually, the heartache that previously consumed any of us that have suffered a loved one's death will unfold into a treasure of memories, and they will be gifts with the passage of time. It might take months or even years of unraveling to find yourself again.

The power connected to giving is immeasurable, and that influence sustains you. Giving of ourselves is the most cherished offering we can present. This book is my gift to you. You can learn your worth. You can do this.

When we realize that material things are fleeting collections of once and will not sustain us in our darkest moments, we will embrace the life we have in a positive, productive way. I still hope that death would take a vacation.

# Acknowledgements

In this fractured time of home and hearth and heart, when the divide seems impossible to cross and the bridge you cannot see, you hold steadfast to all you have. Trust the process, look up and pray. Lean into your pain for a second or two. The truth is, all is not lost nor gone away. You'll need your strength and courage now. In time, the pain will ease. Look for others to show their love, and they will remind you of exactly who you are....

I would like to thank my husband, Larry, with yet another book, another project. You stand by, supportive, omnipresent, making me believe anything is possible. You have shown more courage than any thousand people, and you teach me every day of our walk together -- you have heart and soul and captured mine long ago.

My friends, you reach out and roll up your sleeves with whatever we are doing. I am so grateful all of you are a part of my life. You bring laughter, playfulness, and such a constant source of love for me – Alexa, Pam, Kara, Stefanie, Stella, Sam (thank you for the validation), Donna, Jenny, Lisa and Liz. I love you all (you know who you are).

And, to all the people who made this book possible, I appreciate your help, your input and hard work, late nights and long days. What special people you are! I thank God for all of you every day.

# Preface

If there is one theme that continually surfaces in my practice, it is the thread that weaves together the common experiences shared by humankind.

It is as if we are all destined to live, (and sometimes re-live), particular events in order to gain a universal knowledge meant to be known to us as individuals. I understand and empathize with others so easily, since I have lived through so many teachings from God and the Universe.

These spiritual "classes" have not always been a golden paved path with fluffy clouds and perfect weather. Quite the opposite, in fact, but they were meant to be so that I could be guided toward my true journey and gain my rightful spiritual post. I survived and learned from each occurrence, and have always found myself stronger and wiser at the conclusion.

This much I know: Sometimes we are the educator, and other times, we are destined to be the pupil. If we can learn and apply the gains of these tests, we are rewarded, no matter how difficult or perilous the previous road may have seemed.

Sometimes all you can do is smile, move on with your day, hold back your tears and pretend you are okay.

Save a seat at the table.

# Chapter One
## A Saturday's Child Works Hard for a Living

I have always felt that my true beginnings were chronicled and cemented by my ancestors. Somewhere within me, I know that my destiny began there, long before I was ever to exist on this plane. I have employed ancestral experts to trace these roots in hopes of making sense of the chaotic mess that I became entangled with, but the results made the already confusing puzzle more of a labyrinth that I now know I may never successfully navigate.

Let's start with what I know for sure…

## A Saturday's Child Works Hard for a Living

### My Paternal Grandparents

My grandparents, Barney and Julia, began their married life after being wed on a country bridge in rural Alabama. Barney was of Native American descent and Julia could trace her Jewish roots back through both Jewish Diasporas, exiled Jews. The bridge was chosen as the place to be unified, as none of the local religious institutions would recognize their association. The following stories were handed down by my father (mind you, my father was like a character in Oliver Twist called the Artful Dodger, leader of a gang of juvenile pickpockets who would not know the truth if it stepped up and introduced itself). But as the story goes, my grandfather Barney was a sheriff in the Deep South. Actually, after searching many records, turns out he was a night watchman, a noble profession; a far cry from a badge and a gun. Barney and Julia moved around often. I do not ever remember meeting Barney. He died before I was born. My mother loved Julia. Julia was a kind and gentle soul, a true nurturer that one. Julia died sometime after I was born and before my younger sister arrived. It was a span of about five years. My memories are vague but good ones of her.

### My Father

I am going to refer to my father as "Mills" throughout this Memoir. This is how my mother referred to him. She believed this man did not deserve the respect of a first name and would always make a face whenever he was mentioned as if she just swallowed castor oil.

My father's role, as negative as the experience was for anyone involved, was impactful throughout my entire life. It is here I learned instinctively that through adversity comes strength. From strength, growth can happen. As much as I do not want to glorify him in any manner, I, at least, have to flesh him out. He set off the chain of events that was to become my childhood experience. It was the beginning of a very valuable lesson.

From Barney and Julia coming together, they produced eight children, one of which eventually became the man who fathered me, Barney, a.k.a Mills. I know little of his upbringing, only knowing bits of the person he became. Now, the Artful Dodger as it were, told me he was the seventh son of the seventh son. Later I realized this was from folklore stating the seventh son of a seventh son would be given special powers which translated to me in my later years he hated women! Actually, the truth is my father, Barney, was the fifth son of eight children, three of which were girls. He was the youngest. At least that part was true.

**Here is what I know now:**

I grew up with no father. Did I have one? Yes. My parents were married. My father exited our lives early and never came back by choice. I am not referring to those who have lost their dads through death.

I can always tell when children are fatherless. Where the fathers are not present or accounted for, if you press hard enough, they are hiding a deep well of pain that eats at them. It makes them survivors. It becomes a chess game.

These survivors are very much aware of the moves and rules of the chess game that once was their family unit. When they are young, they are chess players ready to knock any family opponent pieces off the board and move in for the kill because they are starving for love and attention. The fear of abandonment is palpable.

What could I possibly mean by that? I am one of those survivors who felt the only permanent thing in my life was myself. You will never understand unless you have been there. An adult, with help, will still have scars from the wounds of divorce and separation. I have worked on healing continuously throughout my childhood and most of my adulthood.

To the fathers or dads that might be reading this today: your children are not a chess game, and they are not your pawns. What I needed and was not allowed was someone to fight for me. It robbed me of a normal childhood.

If you are thinking about becoming a dad or are a dad, be present and accounted for because children need your love and protection. They need your gentle but firm hand, ordinary routine moments when you have asked them about their day, to read them a story before bedtime and to wipe their tears when the world is unkind.

A fatherless child has only shreds of normalcy.

My Maternal Grandparents

My grandparents, Loyd Biggs and Ada Alice Easter, were married January 9, 1923. Loyd was 21 and Ada was 18. They had seven daughters and two sons, and lived in a house my grandfather Loyd built in St. Louis, Missouri. They were of meager means and very old school.

My grandfather Loyd listened and my grandmother Ada screamed about everything. My memories of my grandmother were loving and kind and one of the most decent individuals of my lifetime as my grandfather was towards me, also. My grandfather played a Hawaiian steel guitar, self-taught and would sing to me in my young years and I loved the sound of his voice. It made me feel safe and special. Later in my life, I came to realize he was prejudiced and a religious zealot and was fierce when serving up the Bible.

**Here is what I know now:**

It is relationships that are the most important thing, not material things.

The path to better living is in developing the compassion and space to love. If we choose only to invest in the relationships that benefit us, that is not love. It is selfish. People were created to be loved. Things were made to be used and to make life easier.

The reason the world is in chaos is that things are loved, and people are finding themselves used. The problem stems from dissatisfaction, so things will bring only a brief satisfaction. It never lasts, it is never enough, we crave more. It is like the closet that is full and the heart that is empty. It creates a deep, dark hole.

You want people around offering the opportunity for you to love, not the love that expects something in return but pure, unselfish love.

My Mother

My mother, Betty, hailed from the Midwest. She was beautiful and was one of two crowned princesses of her clan, complete with valedictorian credentials and a surprising air of sophistication. Her childhood, for her time, was somewhat normal even though in that pocket of time, girls were still expected to marry and have babies and prided themselves on their housekeeping skills. So, for her not to only read and write her speech, she was in what they called the Pen and Scroll (usually a club exclusive to males) which in the 1940s was a big deal. I don't know much more about her childhood except that my grandparents argued a lot but that was seen as normal for that day and time. They were very poor.

Betty graduated from Normandy High School in 1945 as Valedictorian. When Betty shipped off three years later to attend college at Moody Bible Institute, the sky seemed to be the limit. She had received a partial scholarship and had schools lining up for her acceptance. In 1948, the BA programs were three years from start to finish. Today, the same programs are four years.

She was the first female in our family to attend classes for secondary education. Before Betty left for college, she had to remain at home to save money from the time she graduated high school in 1945 until she began her collegiate education in the Fall of 1948. She saved every penny she could to realize her dream and at the same time helped her parents financially by paying room and board as funds were sparse.

Soon after arriving in Chicago, Betty became romantically acquainted with a man named Bill. He was a young, aspiring politician who was making a name for himself on Capitol Hill and he was madly in love with the woman who became my mother. They became engaged, and she stubbornly refused to leave her collegiate post to join him sooner in Washington.

Betty wanted to stay in Chicago and finish her education. She was determined to have a career in a time when most women's aspirations consisted of snagging the first available husband and avoiding a lifetime of dreaded spinsterhood.

During college and afterwards, before leaving for Africa, she worked at Illinois Bell Telephone in Chicago and Southwestern Bell in St. Louis. After Betty graduated from college in the Spring of 1951, before heading to Africa to do missionary work, God had different plans. Instead of spending what I believe was 15 or 20 cents for the streetcar, my mother decided to walk from her rooming house to where she worked as it was a beautiful summer day. Betty considered this great exercise.

That particular morning, Betty walked under scaffolding and something fell from the top of a taller building and hit her directly on the top of her head. People rushed to help and she was transported to a downtown Chicago hospital. As a result of this traumatic brain injury (TBI), brain damaged by physical trauma, she was at risk and ultimately had post-traumatic epilepsy. Twenty-five percent of these victims will experience more seizures in the month following the trauma. There would be long-term consequences for my mother.[*]

In 1951, the medical community decided to put Betty through a series of electroshock and insulin-shock therapies. These therapies were supposed to put her in a coma for one day.

---

[*] Today it is known after a head trauma, it likely reflects generalized excitatory activity in the brain related to the trauma and does not carry an increased risk of epilepsy or ongoing seizures.

Arch Phys Med Rehabil. Author manuscript; available in PMC 2015 Jul 27.
Published in final edited form as:
Arch Phys Med Rehabil. 2014 Jun; 95(6): 1223–1224.
doi: 10.1016/j.apmr.2013.06.002

However, Betty was in her first coma for six months. These therapies were barbaric and experimental at best. No one was quite sure of the outcome.

During the six months, my grandfather sat by her bedside and blamed himself for allowing Betty to go away to school. Once Betty was stabilized but still in a coma, she was transported from a medical hospital in Chicago to a psychiatric hospital in St. Louis. They believed she was not going to come out the same and would be a full-blown epileptic for the remainder of her life.

After the accident, once Bill and his family realized my mother was not going to recover in the manner in which he hoped, love went out the window and he went off to Washington without her. My mother not only had a broken head but a broken heart, for so many reasons. Under different circumstances, she would have managed these painful moments in her life because she would have known they would end. For her, what about the pain that did not end, the overwhelming grief and depression? Betty would never know what it felt like to live without emotional pain again.

Thus began a long and unsuccessful affiliation between Betty and our country's ever-evolving mental health system. She was institutionalized on many occasions that became long-term hospital stays throughout the rest of her life, fed heavy medications, and was a regular hostess to experimental "therapies" that eventually robbed my Mother of her former self. As far as the drugs they opted to give her along the way, many were prescribed, but very few were effective. She became lame in her speech and seemed to develop an early form of dementia, forgetting people and events that should have been easily recalled by someone her age. Her previous vibrancy and intelligence that once radiated from her dimmed to a point of non-existence at times.

My mother lived a simple life at home with my grandparents when she was not hospitalized until the age of 28. During this time, she continued to attend church and led a very quiet existence. The previously mentioned treatments were continued with more time spanning in between the long hospital committals.

After a particularly long hospitalization, and at the urging of my grandparents and her family, Betty decided to set her sights on a husband. She felt ready to pick up in life where she had originally decided to go, and was confident that she was ready for a house and family of her own.

**Here is what I know now:**

A word for Moms.

Sometimes all you can do is smile; move on with your day, hold back your tears and pretend you are okay and know you did the best you could. I was not perfect. I was a teenage mom.

Instead of feeding the fire, balance the passion. For the Helicopters and the Tigers: what I would say to you is let your children dream. Do not make it your fantasy. It has to be theirs because if they want it bad enough, they will be able to achieve anything. Sure, we have to provide the opportunity for our kids and occasionally remind our children that playing the latest mind-numbing game for hours, in the end, will not make a productive adult.

Was I able to let them go when the time came without tucking a checklist of emergency numbers and sometimes money in their bags? Well, I am still working on that one.

What I have come to realize is that quality time is more important than gifts, "stuff" that makes our relationships significant. Instead, it is our simple instinctive presence that becomes the most meaningful. Real conversations are the best!

We hope to preempt every disappointment with comfort when what our little darlings might need most is time to reflect and retrench. What good mother would not want to jump right in and hug their child after their life has dealt them a crushing blow? What we should want is for our kids to have fun, of course, be happy and do well. Our love does not change as they grow into full adulthood. There can be distance and miles, and it dawns on you there are no redos. Maybe we moms want to suppress our inner Helicopter and argue with ourselves against the Tiger. Love your children even if it is at a distance.

For whatever reason, there are ugly gaps between mother and child. Given our frailties, I know all sorts of stories exist, including my own. In some, the pressures of life have shredded the delicate fabric that weaves a family together.

Here is what I know for sure: do not be the person who has all those tears and regrets. I will only say that if it is within your ability to call her, tell your mother you love her. Do not be the one who wishes you could and cannot anymore. Do not be the one that wished death had taken a vacation.

# Chapter Two
## The Cinderella Syndrome

The people who promise never to hurt you are the ones that hurt you the most.

No one deserves a complicated relationship. Do not allow yourself to be ruined by it. You are only going to be as good as the people you have around.

Live as if you were to die tomorrow. Learn as if you were to live forever.

## The Cinderella Syndrome

My parents, Barney ("Mills") and Betty, were wed in St. Louis, Missouri. The church in which they wed was a stately building made of stone not brick. It reminded me so much of St. Louis Cathedral. She belonged to a church group and my father had slithered his way into the group to find his next victim. He had come to St. Louis for work and set his sights on my mother who at almost 29 years of age was more than happy to have the attention. Their courtship was a whirlwind and he was a charmer. He said all of the right things and made it seem as if he was a Southern gentleman. She took the bait and swallowed it hook, line and sinker. They married just after Mills asked my grandfather Loyd for Betty's hand in marriage. By that time, my grandfather was so worn out from my mother's health that he was happy to hand her off, not understanding the ramifications of what was to come. So, all the women in my mother's family busied themselves with making the perfect wedding dress for her and beautiful she was. They were married on October 19, 1956. The reception was at my grandparents' home and I do not remember any stories beyond that except for a few pictures I was able to view.

Up until their wedding day, Mills had presented himself as a perfect gentleman, and quite a catch for a new bride. He had served in the military, held a steady job, and attended church regularly. My mother would never have guessed that he had a well-hidden secret. He was a raging alcoholic.

Mills was not a kind and jovial drunk, and he imbibed daily. He was religiously abusive and belligerent, and soon began having difficulty with steady employment. Often, he would sever these relationships by his own inebriated hands and actions.

Mother seemed oblivious to many of the things he did. Her religious teachings had instructed her to believe that her husband was the head of the household, and she was merely an extension of his needs and expectations.

And so, life, for me, as for so many of us, began cast in the shadows of the ancestral energy laid out in the steps of my family members who walked before me.

I am the second of three children. My older brother, Joey, and I were born in St. Louis in the immediate years following my parents' marriage. Given my mother's age, they felt it was important to start a family as soon as possible. My sister, Jayne*, was born in Georgia, several years later.

Some of you are going to be wondering, How could an epileptic mother give birth to four healthy children? I do not believe this was a question she would have asked because back in those days, women got married and had babies. That is what they did. Plus, my mother was a strong believer God would take care of everything.

Before Jayne, Mills being the Artful Dodger he was, cooked up his next best scheme and began to implement it. How, you might ask? There were several loan companies back then that would give you cash on your signature based on the collateral you wrote down. Apparently, it was a time when people still based everything on your honor and a handshake. So, his collateral was a piece of land with a house and all of its contents. The problem with that was the house, and all of its contents belonged to my mother's parents, Loyd and Ada, where they lived at the time. He forged my grandfather's name. Loyd found out because a debt collector came up the driveway into the yard while he was working on his fruit trees demanding payment or the loan company would seize the house, property and all of its contents. Even in the late 1950's, identity theft had a face even if it did not have a name.

My grandfather was able to prove he did not get a loan, much less sign for one. It was not his signature. Needless to say, my grandfather threw my father out!

A week later, my dad and mom devised a plan and shuffled Joey and me into their car that my grandfather purchased for them as a wedding gift. Mills said we were going to visit his family in the South for awhile. My mother truly believed Mills when he said it had been a mistake or misunderstanding. My mother believed what God had joined together, no man could set asunder so she would not leave her husband and would go wherever he wanted. In other words, my mother took her wedding vows seriously. Even my grandfather could not stop them. Late at night, we headed south for the first of two times.

**Here is what I know now:**

We all need reality checks. Challenge yourself to face reality. Freedom comes with living the truth.

Life is not, in fact, all fun and games. Thus, it is helpful to consider the context of our experiences and how things might affect us.

Sometimes we are pushed forward towards change within and without. Overall, we are influenced to understand our true nature and what we value the most in our personal lives, in friendships and in public.

Grow through what you go through. In a nutshell, we need to slow down and go with the flow rather than always trying to take control and help.

At different times in our lives, we are challenged to face reality. Enabling is fixing a problem for others. In doing so, it interferes with their growth and responsibility. Enablers rush in and remove consequences which in turn give the other parties involved no opportunity to learn valuable lessons and then they are given a free pass.

When asked, proffering wisdom and offering advice, whether the other parties listen and apply it to their own lives, is strictly up to them. Some people do create their storms and then get mad when it rains.

Pray you are brave enough to let your hands fly up and let those adults learn they too can fly and enjoy the ride.

My mother could not draw a line or maintain boundaries. There were times, as a result of her religious beliefs and illness, she would give it the ol' college try. All of our stays in the South were short-lived, and someone else was always left to pick up the pieces. It was brutal and devastating. I have come to understand why in my younger years I made some of the choices I made and how those choices have impacted the people I love.

# Chapter Three
## Roots and Wings

God gave you a gift of 84,600 seconds a day.
What are you using them for?
I came out of the other side of damage.
I was not beyond repair.
Through it all, I have learned important truths.
I want to thank my family for showing me what I didn't want to be.
I could break the cycle. It could end with me.

## Roots and Wings

After months of being down south, my mother, Betty, became painfully aware that Mills had not only lied about never being married before but he had three other children who lived in the same town. He had been splitting his time and money between both families. To add insult to injury, my mother, Joey and I had to move in with my father's family members due to Mills' unstable provisions. Having three mouths to feed was proving to be a difficult feat for him and interfered with the daily goal of drowning himself in a bottle. My mother began to have more and more seizures, which at this time had evolved to bouts of deep depression and despondency. She was clearly overwhelmed and simply could not cope with the life of orchestrating a young family.

When my mother realized this, she called my grandfather, Loyd, from a neighbor's phone to come and get us. She told my grandfather something was terribly wrong with me, she was not feeling good, couldn't feed us and didn't know where her husband Mills went. After the phone call, my grandfather showed up with a cavalry and brought us back to St. Louis.

Once we arrived back in St. Louis, my brother and I had to be treated for severe malnutrition for the first of two times.

According to family members, I was considered "different or retarded" (their words). Stories shared I was a rare infant who did not cry, and people often wondered what might be wrong with me. Questions asked about me: Did I have a deformity or mental delay?

My grandfather took notice that his daughter seemed incapable of providing affection toward her children, and despite efforts made, the state and a pediatrician got involved. The pediatrician was concerned about my non-affect and that

I had not met any major developmental milestones up to that point. The treatment suggested was for people to talk to me, feed me, love on me and try to work with my legs because the pediatrician couldn't find anything physically wrong with me.

What I know now, my mother was terrified to lose us because her husband was philandering with a whole other family and she knew her seizures were returning. My mother was too ill to care for me, yet was possessive and jealous of anyone paying any attention to me, according to family members. She was horrible to my grandmother and would not let anyone come near me. I was not even crawling by the time I was nine months old. Once my mother was hospitalized, my grandfather and other family members began to engage me every night after arriving home from work. My grandfather would work with my legs, sing and read to me in the hope of trying to elicit some response.

I finally began to react to my grandparent's efforts and voices. The answer to my "problem" was simple. I only needed love. I had met every major milestone within a month. Not only could I crawl, I had begun to walk.

Joey was a toddler. He was considered my Irish twin, still in diapers himself. According to family lore, as the story went, back then from the time he began to talk, he was the oldest little man they had ever met. He was wise far beyond his years.

My Dad, according to other people, was traveling for work at the time. The problem was, he was not bringing money back for anyone. Mills decided, after yet another discussion with my grandfather, that we needed to visit the South again and that there might be a job at Ft. Benning or Ft. Rucker. He could not decide but knew there was a job at one of those locations, and my mother was over the moon with the prospect of her husband gaining employment and the idea of making a home for her family. My sister was conceived on this trip. More on that later.

My childhood is best described as a "crash into consciousness," fully aware of fear, tears, and constant malnutrition. Survival would become a key element to my daily life, and that word had not even entered my vocabulary.

Perhaps even from this early point, I was aware of my parent's difficulties and that self-reliance would be essential. My first words were appropriate, "Do it myself!"

People learned Joey and I were inseparable because we were constant companions. If you were looking for one, you need only to find the other.

We discovered with Mills' need for a libation that a corner bar would give you chips and money if you were cute. So, Joey taught me to dance and sing and dance and sing we did for every kernel of popcorn, every bag of chips and every morsel of pickled eggs (I love dill pickles to this day) we could swallow. We quickly learned when we were not busy in the bar dancing and singing that people would throw away perfectly good food in the trash can.

My brother Joey devised a plan and encouraged me to go fishing for food. He would hold me by my ankles or legs so not to knock the trash can over and spill the good food, disgusting when I think about it now, and I would find what we could eat and see if he could clean it off. If it did not smell too bad, we ate it! Now remember I was three or four and my brother was four or five respectively, and some of those trash cans were enormous. If there were some left over, we would run home to our mom up the four flights of stairs, rush in the door to the small dismal apartment and share our catch of the day. We knew our mother was hungry and trying to nurse our sister. There was not a morsel of food in our house, not even a grain of rice. She would light up like a Christmas tree. What stands out in my mind is she would never ask exactly where we got the food. My mom was not neglectful. From time to time, she would call local churches or food pantries, and they would bring us food only to have Mills take it out of the house to sell it for his next drink or share it with some of his friends that were not our family.

**Here is what I know now:**

My mother should have at all costs protected her children. She lived in a time and had an illness with a stigma attached. I do not know how she could have done it differently based on what she had to work with and being born in 1928. In her mind, her marriage was to be kept together at all costs and children were to be seen and not heard.

I am still fighting with myself on the difference between my early reality and what I had wanted it to be. Death is always a gut punch with varying degrees of force and a reminder of our own mortality. I have learned this again and its full impact in the last twelve months. Today is the first anniversary of my mother's death, December 9th. So many people have given me advice on what I should or should not do based on their experience with grief. I received two signs and am going to follow my heart and be true to myself.

As my mother was dying, I kept saying to her when I walked out of her room, "I love you. Save a seat at the table." A couple of weeks ago I heard a song for the first time by Brian Free and Assurance called, "Save a Seat at the Table." It caught my attention. Two days later on television, I heard one line in a movie. Guess what it was? Save a seat at the table! Coincidence? I do not believe in coincidences.

Time waits for no one when you are grieving. Unfortunately, grief does not follow a defined trajectory. What irritates me the most about grief is its sheer unpredictability. The randomness with which it strikes. That is what I found in the twelve months immediately following my mother's death. It does not seem logical or proportionate.

You have to look at what you have lost or did not gain and examine it. Grieving is not a linear process. There is no point A to point B. When you are finally out of shock and in the clutches of grief, a dark tunnel, that is when you need to focus on your emotions and allow yourself to feel. It is insidious. It creeps into your daily life demanding you pay attention.

Either we deal with it, or we get stuck in that memory and time stops. I am not making light of mine or anyone else's pain. It is a long journey back. You are never the same. Your life becomes defined as a past and a present. History does repeat itself. If you think you have it all figured out, I know at some point later in your life, you will be called on to demonstrate whether or not you have learned the lesson. Life either teaches you hard or teaches you well.

For me, it is well with my soul. I am one step closer to acceptance of the before and after. Remember to save a seat at the table.

## CHILDHOOD…

Late on the dishes
Food still on the plate
Momma seems crazy
He is home late
I am in a corner
Crying all alone
Wishing to myself
For a real home

I wasn't the only child to
Ever get a beating
Never treated well
I am not the only
Child
Whose life is a
Living hell

A belt crashes down
One lick two lick
Ten and then twelve
Pretty soon you are
Numb
Your feelings you have
Shelved
All because I didn't
Clean up this place

I have a bed
Not exactly a cozy cot
A scratchy blanket
And no sheets
To get

Laundry not finished

So no dinner tonight
The rest of them all
Eating
Plainly in sight

My clothes aren't the
Best
My shoes never fit
I know what you are
Thinking
I must have been bad
But that isn't the case
Honest to God
I was a misfit
The odd pea from that
Pod

They don't like me
They're mean
That is true
He is always screaming
For what I did and didn't do
Confused
What to do first
Take care of their needs
Or quench my soul's thirst

He tells me I am
Worthless
That I am going to hell
Mom doesn't say much
In fact
Nothing at all

Looking depressed is what
I do best
But surviving this

Childhood
Was and is
My big test

No child should live that life
It should be happy and fun
Every child should smile
And have no real reason
To cry

My little voice grew up
I tried to tell people
What went on
No one would listen
No one heard me
I wondered if I ever
Would be free

I am not a victim
Grown
Full of hope
I have strength and
Abilities to begin again
Because that little girl
That was me
Will win in the end

Joy M. Mills

# Chapter Four
## The Early Years

There have been noticeable absences.
There is always a loud silence when someone
important is missing or lost in dark places.

## The Early Years

Due to Mills' spotty employment record, we were only in St. Louis for a short time after I was born. His military background had left him with loyal friends that informed him of a job offer that took him back to Georgia, where he had been stationed during his active duty and had lived in his childhood. Not knowing at the time what truly propelled this decision to uproot our family, my mother dutifully followed with us in tow.

It was a tumultuous time for all of us, but also a mystical one for me. It was then that I recall beginning to discover my own abilities. Using these gifts, I was able to escape into moments of quiet that seemed to shield me from the never-ending storm that swirled around me in the form of a mother who could not get out of bed for weeks at a time, sprinkled with occasional drunken intrusions from an increasingly absent father.

I recall an incident that resulted in my brother's eyesight becoming permanently damaged. To this day, it is such a vivid memory for me, sticking out because while Mills had arrived home in his usual drunken stupor, he had a rather amorous and affectionate mood about him that night. It ended up being too good to last. I can even remember what he smelled like. He reeked of an old stale bar, a combination of cheap whiskey and tobacco. He quickly became enraged at my mother as she was in the beginning phase of a full-blown seizure. She was trying to put a screaming Jayne down and the inability to connect with him on any level at that moment infuriated him. He did not care. He wanted what he wanted. He tripped over some toy that was left out and he turned into the most-evil man. His face and body changed and a storm was coming, on a scale of about an F4, possibly an F5.

I lived with my family in public housing in a four-story tenement building. Our apartment was so small you had to walk outside to change your mind. As I watched in horror, Mills turned into another person, yanked my baby sister Jayne, less than three months old, from my mother's arms and slung her across the room because she was crying. She hit the wall and fell onto the only other bed, which was what saved her life. I knew to get out of the way because my brother Joey was yanked up in a violent manner as Mills was opening the door with one hand and holding Joey with a death grip in the other with Joey kicking to break free, screaming, "I hate you. Let me go!"

Before Joey was hurled out the door and down the stairs outside of the apartment, Joey screamed, "Sissy Run!" So I did a head dive for the closet because the door was open. I was so scared, I did not breathe, did not move a muscle thinking if I closed my eyes and made myself invisible, he could not see me. My mother was trembling and crying. Even at that young age, I knew a bad seizure was coming for my mom and all I could think of was I could not hear my sister anymore and I did not know where my brother was. My mother was whimpering and crying saying, "Please don't hurt my kids. I'll do whatever you want." These were the only sounds I could hear. I remember thinking, "Is this what dead is," in the mind of a child.

The result of that particular night, Joey was truly hurt which would immediately require corrective surgery to pull Joey's eyes straight and another surgery to be done later in life to stop the trembling of his eyes. Jayne was only stunned. Why it did not kill her, I do not know. For myself, I do not remember talking for some time. I was afraid to. This is what trauma truly is. The only thing I can think of now is that there is a God in Heaven and we were protected, in some weird way, even then.

Somewhere in my vague memory, from the time of leaving my grandparent's home to that date, my sister had been born. I do not know who had us while my mom was hospitalized giving birth to my sister Jayne. But I understood what real fear was. The only two things that would calm me were my brother Joey putting his arm around me and saying, "Sissy it is going to be okay. I'll take care of you," and rocking myself safe (back and forth).

It just so happened to be that Mills' family lived nearby. It was at this time that I remember being first introduced to Mills' siblings. When I initially became acquainted with my grandmother Julia, I recall feeling enveloped with unconditional love for the first time. Hers was the kind of affection that works, heals and loves through love itself.

It was my grandmother Julia who decidedly proclaimed that I had inherited great gifts. Being a woman of great spiritual prowess and known for uncanny predictions, she recognized a part of that in me.

Since our parents were unable to adequately care for Joey and me, we were occasionally left in the charge of other nearby relatives. One such person, Aunt Nadine, would serve us a punishment called, "Sit and Think." This was a welcome reprieve from the beatings and verbal abuse that we had grown accustomed to, and I always oddly appreciated those quiet moments. It was in those moments I learned to observe the world around me and be able to just sit and think.

Stability, for us, was an elusive concept. Looking back at my childhood, I realize now just how much my abilities helped me to survive. During this time, these talents were used both as a weapon and for mercenary purposes, assisting me in the absence of a normal familial structure. Bonded by neglect, Joey and I became inseparable. Those times we were forced to forage for food on the streets or hustle for change, and those moments became a unifying force for my brother and me. Rummaging in dumpsters for leftover food and topping the nights off by sneaking into those local bars to sing and dance for the patrons who might be willing to part with a little money or a soda and chips became some of our many bonding experiences.

As all combustible situations do, our family dynamic finally exploded. My mother, after the final night of horrors for her and us, waited for Mills to leave and after he did, she picked up my sister, collected my brother and me, went to a neighbor's house to use their telephone (the neighbor was sworn to secrecy) and made the long-awaited collect call to my grandfather in St. Louis. My mom told them my brother was injured, I was not talking, Jayne was crying, she was sick again and could someone pick us up. We were seriously malnourished and dehydrated and my sister's cries were barely a whimper.

My mother looked stunned and worried. We went back to our apartment and waited for my grandparents or someone from my mother's family to make the long journey to pick us up. When my mother's family arrived to collect us, my mother was not talking and having grand mal seizures on and off as they hurriedly collected us and our things. The silence was deafening. I just remember my brother and I were very ill and malnourished. We both were vomiting and had chills, fevers, diarrhea and swollen bellies. Mills was walking up swearing at my Uncle saying, "No one is taking my family anywhere." Whatever my Uncle said to my father with his finger in his chest and my aunt holding my baby sister giving her death stare at Mills made him turn around and stop protesting. My aunt was saying, "Hurry along children, keep moving and get in the car." The entire time, my brother held my hand in case Mills came back. We were traumatized.

On the drive back to St. Louis, my mother, Joey, Jayne and I baptized my Uncle and Aunt's brand new vehicle with a constant flow of vomit and diarrhea. It was so bad that at one point, we stopped at my Uncle's sister's house in a nearby state so the car could be hosed out and disinfected. It was still very cold out but we had to have the windows down. Plus, they had to find clothes for all of us, explain to a four-year old, after being potty-trained, why they had to put diapers back on her much less put diapers on her older brother. They had called an old country doctor to try and treat us so we could make the rest of the journey back to St. Louis.

During that time, Mills disappeared, and I would not see him again until I was 27. I would never again see my precious grandmother Julia.

**Here is what I know now:**

Beginnings are beautiful. Starting something new offers excitement and opportunity for change, but often saying hello to the new means saying goodbye to what you knew. When you say hello to a new chapter and you have not closed the door on an old one, you then miss honoring the very best parts of what came before.

Acknowledge the joy and the sorrow. Then step into a new beginning fully present. The other choice would be something else you have to survive.

If you miss what you were uncomfortable with or what was, own it. All of the emotions and the energy that surrounds your beginnings and endings are real. It is crucial; you cannot leave it out of your story. The important thing is to know who you are from the inside out, right now!

You can have a loving relationship without agreeing on everything. If you learn to disagree without being disagreeable, that is wisdom. If you learn to walk hand in hand without seeing eye to eye, that is wisdom.

# Chapter Five
## The Caisson Goes Rolling By

A clairvoyant does not have an incredible way of releasing you from the anchor of your sadness. However, with my age, wisdom and life experience, I do have the ability to listen carefully and empathize and sympathize. What I try not to do is draw comparisons. My personal life and journey have nothing to do with yours. If we intersect, it is because there is a message or a lesson in it. I come to a session honestly and open. It is not my job to draw you a beautiful picture or to scare you to death. Either one of those would be wrong.

A lot of people do not know what a clairvoyant is. My role as a clairvoyant is to provide insight and to give information. I do not read cards, look in a crystal ball, use amulets or any of the other various tools others may use. It is not my job to judge.

We have free will and choice. I do not decide for anyone. Mine is a conversation with the person in front of me. I am the conduit and the messenger and just interpret based on what is happening to the individual at that moment and time and moving forward. I can see obstacles and choices you have that I will not make for you. For instance, if I see a police car pulling you over and giving you a ticket or worse after happy hour, chances are you have used your free will and choice. What happens as a result of your irresponsibility is on you. If someone told me I would get a DUI, I would not be getting behind the wheel of any vehicle after having drinks anywhere.

Some clients want me to make decisions for them. However, I do not do that. My gift is an additional tool to help you figure out your journey if you are standing at a crossroad, making a significant decision or just plain stuck. I am not a fixer but am a messenger. Do not shoot the messenger!

When I am doing my job, I have no personal opinion nor am I a therapist. It is your session, not mine. It is not my job to inflict my opinion on what choices you make.

Skepticism is healthy. A little goes a long way.

## The Caisson Goes Rolling By

Within the day of our arrival back to St. Louis, my baby sister Jayne was admitted to a children's hospital, my brother Joey's hair was shaved off and all of my long curly hair was cut off because of the lice infestation. We were washed with lye soap before we could go into our grandparent's house. As they were cleaning Joey and me, I felt like we were never going to be safe again. It was constant chronic, chaos. This was my normal.

It was November 1963 and my grandparents had set up their brand-new television set in the back room across from the old red vinyl couch. I loved this couch, the smell and the sound. I would rock myself safe. It was home for me.

My mother was asleep upstairs; my brother, sister and I were playing on the floor and my grandparents were watching John F. Kennedy speak on television. I looked up from my game, looked at the TV and asked my grandmother, "Why is that man's head all bloody?" She said, "Joy you are telling a windy. What an imagination you have. That is the President of the United States and he is perfectly fine. There is nothing wrong with his head." It was as if I was slapped. I saw what I saw. As a child, I was typically bullied into silence and submission.

Within hours, my grandparents were whispering to each other. John F. Kennedy had just been assassinated. My grandmother was crying and distraught over his assassination and questioning, "How could that child have known?" It went from being told I was making up a story to them wondering if I was a spawn of the devil. Just shy of my fifth birthday, I was not sure what that meant but I knew it could not be good.

Days later, we gathered around the television to watch little John, John Kennedy salute the Caisson. My grandparents stated they were going to pray and my grandmother reached over, patted my head and said, "We need to pray for Joy, too." This was one of many reasons why as a child, I always felt like a fish out of water and never comfortable in my own skin. It scared me. I thought somehow in verbalizing what I saw, I made it happen.

After Christmas, I remember being in the back room of my grandparent's house rocking on my couch. For Christmas, my grandparents purchased a children's rocking chair in hopes that if I were to have to rock myself safe, it would be in that hard wooden chair instead of on their couch. However, it was my couch. The chair just did not soothe but my doll liked it just fine!

My mother was anxious and out of control, and while nothing in the house had changed, I began to feel a cold chill that made all of my senses become intensely aware that something was about to happen. In that moment, as if it could not get worse, it did.

Within seconds, I heard voices erupting from the kitchen, louder and louder, something crashed and I heard someone say, "Get out of the way!" My grandmother immediately grabbed Joey and me, hid us in a stairwell toward the back of the house and told us not to move, do not come out or open the door for any reason. My grandmother was very stern and was raised to believe spare the rod, spoil the child. We never thought to disobey a direct order from her.

Our mother was running through the house, brandishing a butcher knife from the kitchen and on the attack for anyone that was in her way. Joey and I cowered in the stairwell as we heard the screams and chaos erupting outside the door. I was crying and we were afraid to move. They were yelling, "She has a butcher knife" and my mother was yelling, "I am not going back and you aren't taking my children." The men were yelling they were going to have to get a jacket for her. Much later in life I realized they were talking about a straightjacket. Already suspecting that our mother held particular disdain for us, we thought that she was really looking for us. It took four grown men to finally subdue our mother that night. It would end with our mother going back to the hospital again for a much-needed time away.

Although I was too young to properly process my mother's condition, I knew instinctively that I would be protected and guided by something inside of myself that would keep me and my siblings out of harm's way. It was when we were ripped apart at the end of 1963, I wondered if I could believe anyone over the age of six.

When the news came down that our mother would be having a more extended stay in the hospital, it was delivered by social workers. They had come with officers to our grandparent's home to retrieve us. Our mother, in her unstable state, refused to allow us to stay with our family out of some ill belief that they were attempting to take us from her! My mother signed the paperwork for Social Services to remove her children from those people, my grandparents. She was not aware all three of us would be split up.

The news came suddenly without much time to process, and needless to say, it was a dramatic and devastating scene. We were each placed in separate foster homes. I lost my brother and sister, my best friends, and was catapulted into a frightening new world.

At different times I can remember, in my mother's more lucid moments, she could be the most wonderful person. There were many times when she would come home on a pass from the hospital and we would spend the days together. She would receive a check, we would cash it, and she would take me to Steven's drug store to buy a new toy or treat. These moments were few and far between and my most precious memory is a song that my mother would sing to me in our private moments. She told me she sang this song because on the day I was born, she heard Joy Bells ringing, and that is how she decided upon my name.

"Joy Bells ringing in my heart,
Joy Bells nevermore to part.
Joy Bells ringing down in my soul.
Joy Bells I will be with you
everywhere you go."

I know now that this was my mother's version of the hymn, "Joy Bells Ringing in My Soul."

**Here is what I know now:**

Pain does not show up in our lives for no reason. It is a clear sign something needs to change.

Thirst is a primary physical need, like hunger. It is more than a craving or philosophical inquiry.

If man's soul searches for truth, nothing less than the genuine article, the whole truth will do. No matter how hard or how often the mind attempts to convince the soul, left unsatisfied, the thirst of man's soul results in kind of a spiritual death until you arrive at the whole truth.

I am being led to recognize I have all that I need to complete this journey of a lifetime. Fear does not permanently block my progress; it only arrests it temporarily. Giving a seedling all of the water it requires in its life, all at once, would drown it. Sometimes you have to water a plant one day at a time, a week at a time and for some plants, a month at a time.

There is a message in nature. If you pay attention to what is happening around you, you will understand a lot more about the logic of life. It will mean nothing if you are still in love with your comfort zone. Let's face it; you are not the same individual you were a year ago, a month ago or a week ago. You are always growing; experiences do not stop; that is life!

Changes only occur when we become who we truly are. Here is my point: drama does not just walk into your life. Either you create it, invite it or associate with it. I am not afraid of truth anymore, and I will not omit pieces of me to make you comfortable.

Sometimes the people around you will not understand your journey. They do not need to. It is not for them.

# Chapter 6
## Through the Eyes of a Child

"It is impossible," said Pride.
"It is risky," said Experience.
"It is pointless," said Reason.
"Give it a try," said Heart.

## Through the Eyes of a Child

For the next three years, I was placed in a series of various foster homes in the St. Louis area. From my perspective, it seemed that the homes in which I was placed usually contained uncaring, and sometimes even abusive "parents". These people were the ones that saw fast dollar signs in the opportunity to be a foster parent, being drawn by the appeal of money that the state provides. Back then, there were few prerequisites to this position, and the child monitoring was almost non-existent. It was a breeding ground for further exploitation of children with already horrific backgrounds.

My siblings were scattered to the wind in these homes as well. I can attest that my experiences, while damaging, were at least sparing of some of the things my brother and sister had to endure under the care of their new familial surroundings. Tales from these times shaped our paths into who we would eventually become. Our destinies unfolded as the branches of our family tree became entangled with others' negative emotional intent, not discounting the depravation and separation from what was our true family connection.

Usually, in these homes, you were either very lucky or unlucky (depending on your vantage point) to have other children in the foster homes with you. The fortunate side to this was that the misguided parenting was usually evenly distributed, and less focused on you as an individual. You were herded, so to speak. They did not have the energy or interest to address you one on one, so there were a lot of "family" discussions, which were usually orders given out about cleaning or who was coming or going. Those places are always revolving doors for one reason or another.

The less glowing aspect to sharing your childhood with faux siblings is something that proves an old rule. Children live what they learn. These disconnected environments bred some very cruel children, themselves victims of maltreatment and neglect. In hindsight, my heart bleeds for these children, and I often wonder where they are now.

One of these children, whom I recall specifically as Timmy the Terror, was particularly unbearable. Timmy was born to a drug-addicted prostitute mother, being given up at birth and immediately devoured into an unforgiving system. Most newborns are immediately adopted, but for some reason, Timmy never was.

He left his first foster home at six weeks old with the name those temporary parents gave him. That was the last caring home Timmy ever lived in. The couple was devastated to have him leave, but they were elderly, and generally only took newborns for a matter of days before they were adopted. In the fifteen years they had admirably volunteered their services, Timmy was the only non-adoptee they ever experienced. It broke their hearts so much that they retired.

I know this story so well because Timmy recited it constantly. When you are a foster kid, you always come with a history, which is usually mostly fabricated, and sprinkled with bits of broken facts. Idealization is commonplace amongst throwaway kids, even amongst the most realistic. We are always trying to get back to something or someone, and would proudly boast to anyone who would listen that we were indeed someone's prized possession and that we were loved.

It was because of Timmy's much repeated tale that I ended up taking my first steps into the adult world at the age of 4 1/2. The group of children at our home had expanded to 5, and given that we did not have much in the way of toys or a yard, we were sent to a nearby park several blocks away for unaccompanied daily "play" time, rain or shine. I always knew these trips were ordered out of parental rejection, but I never cared. I would allow myself to play out my fantastical images of being a normal girl who would return home to her real family, and a bountiful feast for dinner. The girl whose family spent time together sharing their meal and recanting the novelties of their day. I had seen this in movies, so that is what happened in other homes, right?

On one of these visits, I minded my business as usual, swinging from the monkey bars and humming a Christmas carol we had learned at school that day. It had snowed a few days prior, and the leftovers of that were melting ice and dirty slush that covered everything it touched.

From my elevated view, I saw Timmy pushing around one of the new boys that had arrived a month before. This boy was one of envy for many of us, since he went on weekend visits to see his "real" mother. We all knew his situation was temporary, and that he would soon be reunited with his blood clan. Timmy did not like this at all, and took every opportunity to let this other boy know it.

The boy, while responding to Timmy's goading, calmly and factually stated that no one loved Timmy, and that Timmy was jealous. This sparked Timmy to begin stuttering his story once again, and while I normally stayed out of things, I had reached a breaking point and yelled from the monkey bars that his story was a lie.

Without warning or words, Timmy charged at me while I dangled from the most unassumingly dangerous piece of playground equipment. Being clotheslined in that manner flung me from the bars into a still frozen chunk of ice, breaking my left arm and resulting in a gash on my thigh that would require 76 stitches to close.

As I laid in the melting snow, I could not help but feel the exhilaration of knowing that my injury was serious, and that meant my Mother would come to see me! Surely, she would! Maybe even out of so much concern that she would round up the rest of my family to visit! Surely, once she had all of us together again, she would realize how unsafe we all were, and bring us all home!

I mentally played out this fantasy as the neighbor walking his dog came upon us, causing quite a commotion, and prompted by the red stained slush where I lay, called an ambulance. I remember the paramedics stating that I was definitely in shock and noted that I had a blissful smile on my face. I certainly did not feel in shock. I was elated! I was going to be reunited with my family! My Mother was going to come and get me!

My only recollection from my actual hospital visit is that no one did come. Not even my foster parents who were only a few blocks away from where the accident happened. I had to spend three days in the hospital, healing from my physical wounds, but I would only survive the feelings of loneliness and emptiness that resulted. I learned the heartache of expectation from a hospital stay.

When I was ready to be released, I was picked up by the social worker who handled my family's case. Since I knew she could tell me where my brother was, I refused to go with her until she agreed to take me to see him. I was grasping at any straw that would provide me a glimpse into anything that was mine, even if only for a few moments.

My intuition told me the social worker was lying when she agreed to this, and I was nonplussed when we arrived in front of my foster home. It was then that I realized I needed to take matters into my own hands. If anything were to be accomplished, it would rely solely on me.

I ran away that night, at age 4 1/2, with my good arm dragging a trash bag half full of every worldly possession I had, and my left leg drudging through the refreezing slush as the army of stitches on my thigh screamed out to stop. I set out to find my brother, not even remotely understanding the distance that truly was between us at the time. How large is a city to a 4 1/2-year old?

Incredibly, my intuition led me in the right direction. I was picked up by two patrolling officers several miles from where Joey was living out his own personal hell. I knew this because I happened to hear one of the officers on the phone with the state children's office.

I spent the night in a small municipality jail cell because, when the officers contacted my foster parents, they stated that I was incorrigible and that they simply did not want me back. There was no social worker available until the morning to retrieve me. I am proud to say, though, that this was the first and only time I have ever spent the night in jail, and this was my closest brush with the law until many years later, in a much different hell I would discover.

Back in the 60s, the foster care system was typical of its time in that it was more about numbers and not reuniting families. It was either all of you or none of you; bonding was discouraged. This is what I know now about the foster care system of the 60s so why would my foster mother come to the hospital to check on her foster child? Furthermore, why would my mother have ever been called?

I was lost and drifting in a system that was awash with inconsistencies and a lack of empathy of the children and the parents taking care of them.

In life, at this time, every step of the way had been extremely hard, riddled with insecurities, lack of support and feeling so unwanted. I always felt like a throwaway child, something to be dealt with and then forgotten. Kids needed counseling and support to cope with the constant change and interruptions in their lives. Think about this for a minute: the loss of parents, siblings and stability…

The trauma a child deals with each and every time they are picked up and placed in a new home is unimaginable to the ordinary person. The insecurity and hollowness this creates. The hopelessness this creates. I do not even have words to describe all of the feelings and psychic changes that are experienced by children who live their lives this way year after year until someone can no longer receive a check from the state and then they are turned out to the streets to survive.

Conversely, those in authority have to make hard choices and still do; taking children from parents who do not deserve them nor deserve the numerous chances they had been given. Law Enforcement/Social Services get caught in the quagmire of what is the best-case scenario for these children to survive and it stands true even today. The biological parents are given time after time to clean up their act while the whole time the children are waiting in limbo shoved about and getting older with each passing year and less adoptable as each year comes and goes. Social Services, present day, does everything possible to reunite the family. The overall goal of the Child Welfare System has always been to maintain safety and permanency for children. Historically, the path of this goal has been riddled with ambivalence.

How could you return a child in one year's time when I had a mother who was hospitalized for three and one-half years at different intervals in her life time? The hell I might have endured given back to my biological father would have been unimaginable.

To add insult to injury, what my mother must have endured having a head injury that cost her everything including but not limited to her children. Imagine the stigma involved.

**Here is what I know now:**

You were born to be real, not perfect.

One way to deal with a desperate situation is to look at it as a necessary or growing experience.

Maybe there is a purpose to it all! Maybe it is not random. Everyone has happiness, heartbreak and sorrow. We all need support, prayer and each other.

In the end, happiness is not absent of problems but the ability to deal with them. Look at what you have and not what you have lost. You have to do hard things to be happy, the things that frighten you, the things other people cannot do for you.

We are at the best of times and the worst of times. Make sure everyone in your boat is rowing in the right direction, not drilling holes when you are not looking.

People decide. God disposes. God is in control. God always has the first move. We may never understand here on earth.

"Depart from evil, and do good; seek peace and pursue it."

~Psalm 34:14~

# Chapter Seven
## Times Three

Jesus said, "Let the little children come to me,
and do not hinder them,
for the kingdom of heaven belongs to such as these."

~Matthew 19:14~

## Times Three

With spring comes new growth but it was not to be that year. After yet another bout with my mother's seizures, another lengthy hospitalization and her divorce from my biological father whom I did not see again until I was 27 years of age, we were returned to my grandparent's house.

My mother in a very excited tone said, "Kids (as if we did not have names), you are going to meet some very special people today. Momma is getting married." She herded my sister, brother and me onto my grandparents' porch to await their arrival. I remember thinking anything has to be better than the winter before and what a winter that was. My sister and brother were still in their foster homes because they had adjusted well to their environments and apparently, I had not.

I went back to my grandparents' home for my own safety. Because no one could handle me, I was allowed to live with them with the stipulation I would not run away again and that Children's Services could make random home visits.

I remember my Grandpa saying, "Your mother is coming home for a visit tomorrow," so I hopped out of bed with a spring in my step that morning. It was breakfast time but I was so excited I could not eat. I promptly sat myself down in front of a window overlooking my grandparent's driveway. It was covered with snow and all of the trees had icicles hanging from every limb as far as your eyes could see. In the mind of a child, it was nothing, but in the mind of an adult, it would be considered pristine and beautiful if you did not have to travel in it. If you did – treacherous.

Then it happened! Hours later, my grandfather came over and knelt down to eye level. He needed to have a talk with me. I knew that look! In a very gentle tone began to speak. "I am really sorry, but Mommy won't be coming home today. The winter storm has made that impossible. It wouldn't be safe." In my mind, it was yet another disappointment and another adult telling me something that was not true.

At that age, I did not understand that weather controlled everything and he did not understand what he had just done. I cried and cried and went into the back room and rocked myself safe. Nothing he or my grandmother said could fix it.

The days passed, and again, with the driveway, which was very long and winding, at least to a very small child, came this little bitty vehicle. Looking back, I believe it was a Volkswagen Bug. It stopped, and out stepped a very tall man and his triplets. The thing I remember most as I was standing on my grandparents' porch was watching them take their leave from the car one at a time with the sun glistening down on their red hats with wide brims and white piping and double breasted white button red coats to match. In my young mind, I asked myself, "Are they rich?" because they all matched. All three wore white patent leather shoes topped with lace bobby socks. They followed behind this very tall man holding each other's hands with a death grip.

They made their way to the front porch. "This is going to be your new dad and your new sisters," my momma said with glee. The look on her face was almost euphoric as if she just won the lottery. My brother and I looked at each other and then looked at Jayne and then all looked back at each other again trying to understand what this meant. New family? Every time we heard "new family," it meant we were packing a bag again, going to have to say goodbye and get into that Volkswagen Beetle car.

After introductions had been made, the adults went into the other room and left us to get to know one another. Actually, they were planning their nuptials for that very week. The triplets removed their hats and coats, neatly put them down on the sofa and with that, the oldest triplet turned on her heels, balled up her fists, looked directly at me and said, "We don't like this anymore than you guys do. If you keep looking at me like that, I am going to punch you right in the face and I am going to tell my dad you started it." My brother promptly stepped in front of my sister and me and said, "You will have to deal with me first." She then relaxed her fists and that was my introduction to the triplets.

The next thing we knew, we were all being packed up because my mom and my stepdad had married and purchased a home. We were excited because we would not have to move anymore but that meant we had to live with the triplets. Imagine the small car with six children and two adults. The house felt smaller still.

Adding to the chaos, the deal was sealed with the birth of another baby, a boy. They named him Daryl*. My mother was so pleased to present her new husband with his only son. The triplets paled in comparison to him.

They registered us for school and I had tested out of the grade they wanted to put me in. The triplets were left behind even though we were the same age. My stepfather thought somebody had certainly made a mistake or some kind of error but for whatever reason, the school did not change what they had done. He made me feel like a pariah everywhere I went. I have not forgotten those feelings to this day.

I learned being too honest was not a good thing. I did not lie but learned to just be quiet. I just wanted to disappear. Looking back at it now, I felt disposable and was disposable. I guess I projected that outward as if I drew a circle jutting out around me saying, "This is my space and you stay in yours." I could have made friends but I just did not trust the kids or the adults around me because as soon as I did, someone was packing my bags of the little belongings I had and telling me it was time to go.

I had a Barbie doll. Even by today's standards, it was a collector's item. It was my prized possession. It was the one thing that survived all of the moves and everything I had been through. She meant everything to me. One day, I was playing with my brother Joey's radio and accidentally broke a knob off. My brother went to my stepfather and asked if he would fix it. He fixed it all right, and fixed it he did. He screamed out my name in his drunken stupor and told me to bring my Barbie doll with me and present myself. Deep inside I knew the only thing I loved would be taken away from me and not just for a minute. My stepfather ripped her head off and sliced her up into little pieces. He looked at me and told me to bring her clothes and said, "You won't need them." He cut up all of her clothes and into the trash can they went. I was devastated. Joey had no idea he would unleash a monster in asking for help. From that moment on, I told myself I would never be dependent on anyone who smelled and acted like my stepfather. To this day, I have him to thank for that important lesson.

**Here is what I know now:**

Overly critical people whose happiness comes first do not respect boundaries or you.

Have you ever had the disconcerting experience of being accused of something you have not done and it turns out the person is, in essence, working up a case against you because they have done something to you that you do not know about yet? They may feel guilty about something they have kept hidden.

It is as if they need to create a situation to justify in having done what they have done. The joy of projection. When someone is projecting, it is really about how they feel or what they have done. You get accused of acts that are entirely out of left field, or innocent behavior gets twisted around to suit them.

People like this apologize for the misunderstanding or try to force you to apologize. Okay, I thought about it, but wonder what is really behind this. Then, it all comes out. Their secret, the feelings they masked find a way to show themselves by creating uncomfortable situations. It is only a means to an end for them.

They try and change the story by saying, "I wasn't there," or they recast themselves as a victim by smearing someone else or by throwing in yet another story to distract from the real issue.

It is critical for us to know ourselves and to be able to discern where we end and others begin. When we do not, we are inclined to absorb the blame and be quick to take ownership of other people's feelings and behavior.

Projection invariably can, in particular when we are on the receiving end, cause us to have the whole mind game feeling. Are we living on the same planet or even talking about the same thing?

What wears us out is when we end up defending ourselves, explaining and re-explaining, reassuring and being super mindful of our behavior to keep the peace. It will steal your peace.

Remember, when someone is projecting, it is about how they feel and what they have done. You are responsible for you. Take care of yourself. It is okay for you to be happy. You are not responsible for someone else's happiness or what is believed to be true.

After all, there are two sides to every story. I believe the truth is always in the middle.

# Chapter Eight
## Out of the Mouths of Babes

Feelings are real and legitimate.
Blind faith and trust leave a legacy
of brokenness.

Childhood hurt deep in a place
I thought I would find peace.

## Out of the Mouths of Babes

Each of us had a tenuous relationship with the other. The dynamic created by the collision of everyone's previous experiences was one of a psychotherapist's dream. Countless billing hours of laying out the daily revulsions of that environment.

Despite everything, we managed to consolidate as a family unit. We were Nightmare on Elm Street's version of the Brady Bunch, shoved into every nook and cranny of the smallest four-bedroom home you could ever imagine. Not only was there limited space in all realms, but also a lack of many basic resources, such as food and shampoo. This created a competitive atmosphere to say the least. For instance, my hair had grown out since our arrival from the South. It was flowing down my back, naturally curly.

The problem was we did not have a shower; we had a bathtub with a faucet. Since shampoo was not available, we were told a bar of soap was good enough. I washed my hair one night a week. Saturday night bath and I washed it as well as any girl of six or seven. The underneath got soap matted, a true rat's nest - knot after knot after knot. It made me cry. It hurt to try and get a comb through it.

Now, my stepfather did not like tears and he said he was going to give me something to cry about. Out came the pinking shears (scissors - blades of which are saw toothed and leave a zigzag pattern instead of a straight edge) and he chopped it off with one cut and then he had to "even it out." He then spun me around and said, "Now for your bangs." Maybe he had a fetish for cutting things with sharp objects. He said in a vengeful voice, "Now, you won't be needing shampoo, problem solved."

With bangs uneven and inch long hair, off to school I went. The real haircut came when Social Services arrived to collect us again and decided my hair definitely needed to be evened up at a beauty school. I wonder today if parents realize how deeply they can wound their young children because there is power in words and even more pain in action.

We were consistently in a state of someone being in trouble or punished. Oddly, we persevered. Each of us finding our own unique way of coping or comforting. Alliances were formed and enemy lines drawn. Manipulations were a daily means of survival, all of us competing for the limited guidance that our overwhelmed and preoccupied parents had to give. In hindsight, we were all so starved on every level.

Quite possibly, out of necessity, I began to rely heavily on what I had begun to call, "My Gift." By then, I had realized that not everyone had these "feelings" or "inclinations," and I confided these things to very few people. My brother, sister and I were different, singled out and made to feel expendable. In that clan, you formed small circles of trust where you could.

I began to pick up on smaller things that would eventually lead to me being more tapped into events of magnitude. Sometimes, this would be as simple as a punishment from my parents and others could be as serious as John F. Kennedy's assassination.

I had been restless for days, hair on end constantly and trying not to pace like a mustang before a violent storm. I decided that this was not something resulting from my personal actions and that this must be something bigger. From experience with my instincts, I grew fearful. Knowing that a train is going to hit you, but not when, is somewhat terrifying to anyone, much less a small and insecure child.

Something was brewing and it was big. I felt like something was coming to get me like the boogie man setting out to steal me in the middle of the night (even that was somewhat appealing to my childlike mind of constantly comparing how someone's grass was always greener than mine). This feeling had weight and sat like an anvil on my chest, making it feel like a chore to breathe. Add the sensation of my stomach migrating to my throat and it was nearly impossible not to feel claustrophobic, even in the most open of spaces. As the days ticked by, all of this only intensified.

Then the picture show started. That's what I had dubbed it, anyway. It was as though a movie reel spun an opaque story in front of my eyes. The only problem is that this was not always a chronological account of events, so I was left to wait for the true interpretation.

I saw rain against a window and dark skies that grew darker. I envisioned an ominous and twisting wind tunnel like the one from the movie, "The Wizard of Oz," tearing down a street and taking anything in its path along with it. I thought I remembered it being called a twister; I had no true knowledge of what that actually meant. I remember thinking that a battle of witches would soon occur, with flying monkeys and all. I would finally get a front seat to Dorothy and that adorable little Toto and that is precisely what I reported to my family!

My mother shooed me away with an annoyed worry as I announced this in our kitchen that morning. As I defied her and said I was not telling tales, she was quick to cross the room with an open palm that connected loudly and left a lovely shade of blush on my left cheek, just in time to leave for school.

My brother Joey walked quietly alongside me to school, offering the assurance that his strong and steady presence always catered to me. Finally, he spoke up, and confidently proclaimed that he believed me. He said he would be on "Big Brother" duty all day, and keep a look out for any trouble or better yet, adventure!

I nervously bit my dirty fingernails all through class during that day, as I was certain the anticipated events would unfold at any moment. Imagine my disappointment as I took the sunny walk home, without a cloud in the sky. I began to contemplate the metaphorical interpretation of the movie played out in my head as I fell onto my cot in the room that I shared with my three other sisters.

It was my turn to control our small radio that day, so I can say with certainty that the last song played was, "The Last Train to Clarksville" by a new band called The Monkees. They had just finished one of the last verses, "And I don't know if I'm ever coming home," when the disc jockey came on air suddenly advising everyone to seek shelter, followed by a blaring emergency signal, both on air and from an eerily close location nearby our home.

I heard my Mother yelling from below in a panic-stricken voice. She was not accustomed to leading the charge of us children, but my stepfather was gone, filling in on the night shift. That is what he said anyway. From what I later learned, most of those nights were not spent toiling away to support his family, but rather, on the stools inside of two local taverns that he frequented. Rotating between them when he had worn out his welcome, coming back around when time had cooled the jets of one place and started fires in the other.

The eight of us huddled in the cramped basement. I carried baby Daryl, who was seven months old, down the stairs and handed him off to my mom. Next, Joey and I dragged a double mattress down the stairs and placed it on top of us, and waited in near silence for the impending natural doom that swirled outside. Mother and the other girls began to whimper and cry, huddled in a corner of the earthy room. We sat there, time suspended, the slightest sound causing us to tense, bracing ourselves for the worst.

And then we heard it. I knew what to expect only from my visions, and was very proud that I had identified the freight train comparison solely from those cinematic visualizations. The tornado was louder than expected, and I was surprised when we were not sucked straight up, but remained there together amidst the foundation of our home, clutching closer together as a group than we ever had, terrified to lose what little we did have.

The tornado came through as we sat in complete darkness, listening to the crash of our furniture and the rattling of the windows above. Mother was a wreck. Even in the darkness, she was easy to spot. Face as white as a sheet and the metal of the belt buckle she wore around her neck clicking as she shook with the fear of a hunted animal. Even through all of the banging and crashing, I knew we would be all right, and I kept repeating these words of assurance over and over to my family.

The five minutes it took for the tornado to pass seemed like an eternity. I envisioned that I would have a new rearranged neighborhood once we emerged. An eerie silenced enveloped the air as we ascended from the basement stairs, and it was all a very confused mess. The stillness was broken by the sound of an ambulance wailing in the distance.

On the evening of Wednesday, January 24, 1967, an F4 tornado hit the north end of town in St. Louis killing three people, injuring 216 and causing heavy damage to businesses, homes, power and gas lines. It was an unusually warm day for January, reaching 65 degrees. Eight other tornadoes struck Missouri that day. There were 32 tornadoes in all, occurring from Oklahoma to Wisconsin.

The tornado dominated national headlines for days. The damage to homes, businesses, and the power and gas lines was catastrophic to our small Midwest city. The neighborhood we lived in was off limits due to the live wires from the fallen electrical posts. No one could get in and no one was allowed to leave. After the shock wore off, the days were spent cleaning up the various treasures that found their way into our yards from only who knows where.

Several homes on our street had been completely demolished. Our house was one of the few with a roof still on it. One of the fatalities had lived a few doors down from us, and my mother was completely paralyzed from everything that had happened. She could not get herself off of the sofa for anything other than to adjust the antenna on the battery powered radio that was providing non-stop updates of the devastation.

One day, while I was volunteering to help in a nearby yard, I was surprised to see my mother approaching. Naively thinking that she had come to help, I broke into a big smile to welcome her. It was only when she broke into a sneer as she came closer that I realized I was in some sort of trouble.

She began by grabbing me by the ear, and hissing about God keeping everyone safe. By then, my mother had graduated to a full blown religious fanatic and you never knew how or when she was going to interpret one of your actions as a deadly sin. It became clear what she was referring to, when she began to say that I made a deal with the devil for "My Gift".

I was scared, and crestfallen, for I had only shared what I sensed in hopes of keeping my family safe. My mother did not see it that way, and informed me of the penance that I would need to pay in order to be pure in the ways of the

Lord. Apparently, my mother felt that the Lord believed little girls scrubbing floors is the fastest way to redemption.

**Here is what I know now:**

Chaos should not be the status quo for the majority of your life. Does it matter in the long run? When you are observant, you notice those that enjoy fighting with someone or themselves.

The antidote:

Zoom in so you can see things in your life for what they are. It could help you avoid negativity, unpleasantness, overly dramatic people and those that utter untruths non-stop for no known reason (the ones with lying handicaps). You should be puzzled by those who do these things with such frequency.

The lesson:

Anything you resist persists. Be an observer, not a perpetrator. It is not necessary to react to everything. If someone repeatedly comes to you with catastrophes, give yourself a window of time. Resist the urge to jump into their pity parties. Kleenex is not free, and you will not be either.

The answer:

Maybe we should all take an inventory of those in our lives that leave us feeling stressed and unhappy. Realistically we cannot completely remove all toxic relationships. Change how often you spend time together. It is similar to a tornado coming. When you hear the warnings and sirens, you are supposed to go to safety. Minimize your time. Steer conversations somewhere else. If that is not possible, then find the nearest exit or shelter.

Usually, dramatic people looking for upset are looking for anything to ease pain and prove they are okay. They want to validate themselves. They have an answer for everything.

Your role:

If you cannot be honest and tell people what you think without clearing the room, what is the point? Pain or frustration is sometimes an indication we need to learn to set better boundaries. Being honest and having integrity is a valuable asset - communicate.

There is peace in the basement (In the Midwest, we have basements. When a tornado is coming, you head downstairs for safety):

When you do not respond to melodramatic people, it dies out. When you react to it, it adds fuel to the flame. How do you choose to be silent when all you want to do is scream?

The first step is to recognize it. If chaos has always been the word of the day, your past is just a lesson, not a life sentence. Today lies new possibilities. Today you decide the direction of your life.

# Chapter Nine
## On My Own

Distance

In the night, I sleep alone
Dreaming in detail of a place called home.
My fears aside, a light I see,
Knowing full well, there is only me.
I awaken to the sounds of the morning's rush,
No human "Good mornings."
No gentle touch.
It's a lonely existence, this time in my life,
Heartaches around cut like a knife.
I smile for the world, it's expected of me,
The real self is what they really never see.
I hold a dream inside my heart,
Knowing it will come to pass if I play it smart.
Time ticks by, my tears do fall,
Hoping the phone will ring with that special call
For someone to save me…

## On My Own

It was shortly after the tornado when my mother had another episode, the result of which precipitated her exit once again to commit to a hospital stay. To sum it up, this was a very confusing and frightening time for all of us. After less than four years, my mother had managed to get married, get her three children back, gain three stepchildren, have another baby and lose her marbles again.

It was time for a medication adjustment and what everybody around her would call, "a long rest." Now I know her long stays were in the psych ward at the St. Louis Insane Asylum on Arsenal Street in St. Louis, Missouri. It reminded me of the old 1948 movie, called "The Snake Pit." This film was a detailed chronicle depicting a woman's stay in a mental institution.

Which meant that my stepfather was faced with the task of raising seven children for an undetermined amount of time. We had never taken much precedence in his normal schedule, so how was he going to fit all of us in under such extraordinary circumstances? This came at a time where it was a common assumption that fathers of any sort were somehow incapable of single parenthood, no matter how limited. Fathers babysat their children then only for the mother to run to the market and back.

In the end, we were again all broken up and scattered to the wind. My stepfather returned the triplets to their mother who lived in another state, which left the remaining four of us alone. It seemed that no one was standing in line to immediately take the remaining four of us. My mother's brothers and sisters were quick with the excuses and did not want any part of taking on four children. They claimed their homes were already too full or there just were not enough resources to provide for all of us. My mother's parents had fallen ill and were much too frail to attend to four children, some heading toward adolescence, and one still in diapers.

Our situation quickly deteriorated, especially for me. I was no longer allowed entry into the foster care system, for the word, "incorrigible," was stamped throughout my records folder nearly as much as my given birth name.

One of my mother's sisters did make a phone call to Social Services because my stepfather quickly abandoned any ties with us and ignored the fact that we were home, or possibly in need of anything. The truth was that my stepfather really did not want to give up the four of us because my mother's Social Security disability money was involved.

Joey and I huddled around our younger siblings in those confusing weeks. School was out of the question because there would be no one to care for Daryl and Jayne. I can proudly say that due to those circumstances, I can craft a cloth diaper out of just about anything.

I remember none of us knowing how to cook, but scouring the kitchen for ingredients of something, anything, that could provide nourishment for the four of us. Known for looking at the bright side of things, Joey spun a narrative that enabled me to think of it as playing house, and that we were special because we were given these circumstances. I would have almost believed him if it were not for the constant grumbling of my stomach and the day the lights went out, literally.

Since we had not gone to school, I suppose suspicion began to arise that we were all no longer present to the entire neighborhood, much less our classes. One of my aunts had made a call. Our electricity had been turned off that day, and I remember waking up and going into the bathroom for the first time that morning, and nothing happened when I flipped on the light switch. I panicked when I heard a knock at the front door. I peered out the curtain and it was a woman who looked nice enough. We were so hungry we opened the door, welcoming her into our dark world and home.

All it took was a police officer to find my stepfather smelling like Falstaff beer down at one of the neighbor's houses, and his denouncement of us as his children to send everyone off packing. Since no one could see very well within the house, we were hurried in what was already a rushed situation. I remember desperately attempting to locate my favorite doll, to no avail. When I protested the calls of the social worker, I was carried downstairs by the attending police officer, empty-handed.

As I stood on the front porch, I noticed a third car pull up outside my house. It belonged to my Aunt Hilda, one of my mother's younger sisters. She had called the state, and explained how no one in the family could step forward to take such unruly children, especially me. She went on to explain my "incorrigible" nature, and suggested that perhaps I was the reason for my mother's current condition. In her eyes, she thought of us to be a bunch of wild hooligans, running the streets, and needing some tough love.

The social worker must have found Aunt Hilda's words believable because my siblings and I were taken to Social Services and separated from there. They were taken in one vehicle headed towards a temporary foster home, and I was headed for a concrete crib, otherwise known as an orphanage.

**Here is what I know now:**

The fact that there is a highway to hell and only a stairway to heaven says a lot about anticipated traffic numbers.

If you have forgiven someone, does that not mean you have moved beyond it and let it go?

The best thing to hold onto in life is each other. God does not promise tomorrow. Why do people bring up the past over and over? With it comes the same angst and a fair amount of grief.

My prayer is that we can get beyond all of the finger-pointing and blame without anything traumatic being the impetus. We have to have confidence in our personal relationships. Unfortunately, other people's ideas of what that is does not always match up with reality. Then choices have to be made.

Just as a candle cannot burn without fire, we cannot live without a spiritual life or God. After all, it began with love and forgiveness.

# Chapter Ten
## Summer Camp It Ain't

Find yourself and be that.
Turn wounds into wisdom and strength.
Remember, in doing something differently,
it may surprise you.
Happiness is on the inside.

## Summer Camp It Ain't

The first thing that struck me was this place looked like a palace, complete with art and a grand piano. I had never seen anything like that in all of my eight years and remembered thinking, "This is gonna be fun!" My enthusiasm was short lived but for the moment I was thinking, "I get to live here!"

They quickly seized my little plastic bag of all my worldly possessions. They made an intercom call to a woman named Ms. Rita who was going to be my dorm mom letting her know, "She's here," as if I did not have a name. At that moment, I realized I was truly alone.

The time I endured there was a blur of pain, isolation and adjustment. Ms. Rita instructed me to walk behind her, advising me that everyone walks in single file and there are rules here. I can still hear the click of my shoes on that floor as she led me to the place where I would sleep indefinitely.

I was saying, "I want my mommy." Her response was, "Nobody likes a crybaby." I did not shed one more tear in that building that anyone could see.

I was told I would have a room to myself. That may have been my eight-year old reputation coming through the door before me. Now keep in mind, I probably weighed fifty pounds soaking wet, but I still managed to be known as a flight risk.

The room I was assigned was sterile and clean with a dingy, rose-colored bedspread they called pink. A hospital room would have been more inviting. First thing Ms. Rita showed me was how my bed was to be made every day by ripping it apart. I had to demonstrate for her how I could make a bed. She then showed me how to do it properly, which is where I learned to do hospital corners. I watched intently since I never had a complete sheet ensemble and did not want them taken away, or worse yet, have to share if I made a mistake.

The next rule was there were to be no watermarks in the bathroom sink, which meant you were provided a towel, washcloth and face cloth. You were to use your face cloth to wipe up the sink after brushing your teeth. The cloths were washed about three times a week. To put it bluntly, they took away my home, my parents and my siblings but I received in its place toothpaste, toothbrush, towels, real shampoo and personal items I never had before!

Ms. Rita pointed to the shiny white floors and said, "No marks will be left, or made on these floors, under any circumstances." If so, it was a demerit which meant a treat or privilege would be taken away. A treat could be a bag of chips, a can of soda or once a week playtime. A privilege would be watching television or coloring in a very tiny room.

My first lesson in how a bank worked was at this orphanage. Every child who lived in this home had a concession account for the once a week treats which meant I had to learn to add and subtract quickly. If you used up the money, you would not be able to buy any treats until the first of the next month. Likewise, if you received a demerit, it was taken away. I thought I was rich and had struck the mother lode! Then, reality set in. Nobody was coming for me.

The "incorrigible" label followed me and they made sure I never forgot it. There was not much to cling to but we were allowed a few precious possessions. I had a St. Bernard stuffed animal with a barrel around his neck. I quickly realized the barrel opened up, so I journaled as much as any small child could, hiding secrets inside his barrel, believing he was going to keep them safe. Turned out nothing and no one was safe from Ms. Rita, including the note I wrote stating, "I hate Ms. Rita." I can still see her holding my dog and that stupid note today. Ms. Rita snorted like a bull. I had not seen anything yet.

The dustup was yet to come. The fallout from that was no paper, pen, crayon or pencil for me in my room. In my young mind, I wondered, was that a lifetime sentence without any writing utensils? She also gave me a demerit. I REALLY did hate Ms. Rita.

Dear God, I am sorry. The funny thing, Ms. Rita said she was going to teach me about hatred. She did.

In the orphanage, they have something called a shoe closet. I had outgrown the only pair of shoes I had, which came from Social Services. My feet were measured; I was told to choose from one of two shelves, one pair. My eyes went straight to a pair of red shoes. I thought they were the most beautiful things I was ever allowed to have. To me, they were equivalent to Dorothy's. I was so excited about those shoes, I came down the hallway and wouldn't you know it, there was Ms. Rita, with her arms crossed. My beautiful new shoes, clickety-clicked when I walked. She stood there with her arms crossed, until she saw me, that is. She outstretched her arm and pointed. I turned to see what the fuss was all about. To my dismay, there were black marks all the way down the hall I had just proudly strutted.

Another dorm mother spoke up for me, "The child has to have shoes." The decision was that they would be worn if I was going someplace "nice," as if my social calendar was full. I was otherwise not allowed to have them. I was provided an ugly, but suitable pair of shoes to wear. I was made to clean the scuffs off the floor as best I could with a rag and no cleaning fluid. I was being taught a lesson. The irony being, they gave me those beautiful shoes. Ms. Rita promptly took those red shoes away, placing them out of my reach, on the top shelf of my closet. I waited until bedtime, scooted a chair over from my desk and obtained my prized new shoes. I was nothing if not defiant. I fell asleep clutching those precious, red shoes. They were mine.

In the morning, lights on, Ms. Rita found me with my prized possessions. She walked out and came back with a long pair of scissors. She cut up the shoes and tossed them in the trash, satisfied with her victory over me. I learned two things that day. Do not trust adults and do not get attached to things.

**Here is what I know now:**

You have brains in your head. You have feet in your shoes.

Our families frame our understanding of who we are and who we can be. We are what our thoughts have made us. Each person that I have encountered in my life has taught me something about myself. The key is to be centered and not placing too much emphasis on the need for acceptance. I am finding peace even while my heart is still in pieces.

When you learn from the past and can let it go, it is easier to attract what you do want.

I want to encourage everybody out there to keep going, keep moving and keep praying. Over time, you reset your expectations of the possible. Perfection is an illusion.

Some would say every day is bright. In our youth, we thought we could do almost anything. When you dreamt of starting a business, creating inventions that solve real problems or becoming a doctor and curing cancer.

Here is what I have found: We live in a broken world. If you give up when life is not going well, you never learn to trust anything or anyone, not even your own judgment.

Start losing yourself in your hopes and dreams. Start losing yourself in your goals and aspirations. Lose yourself in fun. Find something in your life that is special and then live it, love it and become it.

We all want to feel happy. We all want to avoid feeling pain. That is what makes hope exciting. It divorces us from the moment and projects us immediately into something better.

When you believe you can be happy regardless of what is gained or achieved, you open your eyes and find reasons to feel and share the joy.

# Chapter Eleven
## The Two Faces of Ms. Rita

One of the most dangerous roads to go down is the what ifs.

This last year has led me on a journey that has been an overwhelming journey of sifting and sorting the good and the bad memories. The complex childhood memories and the complicated adult realities.

As of this writing, I am remembering both my mother's flaws and knowing she was capable of kindness and love.

## The Two Faces of Ms. Rita

What I did not understand, nor would they have shared with a small child, was that trial weekends occurred prior to being transitioned home or out of the system.

Here is the coup de gras of my stay at the orphanage. One Saturday morning at 9:00 a.m. Ms. Rita came into my room and instructed me to pack a suitcase to include a nightgown, one change of clothes, socks, underwear, pajamas and a toothbrush and toothpaste in a plastic baggie (the fold over kind). All with my name written on it. She barked instructions saying, "This better all come back with you."

She continued, telling me not to wash my hair, warning if I returned with a rat's nest she would not hesitate to cut it out again. She then checked my suitcase, tore it apart and made me repack it. I did, with that one change of clothes and that one pair of shoes. Not the red ones. She took care of those.

Ms. Rita, having the weekend off, escorted me through the forbidden set of double doors where children are not allowed to go, down the long hallway and promptly deposited me in the lobby. She pointed at this very, large blue winged-backed chair and told me, "Don't you move from this spot." She said, "We'll be watching you." That thought did not cross my mind; I was so excited my mom was coming.

I did not start to cry until I heard the lunch bell ring. Then I sucked it up and thought maybe she was late. I sat there. I did not move from that chair. By the time the dinner bell rang, it had begun to get dark outside; the weekend dorm mother had returned to collect me. She patted my hand and explained I needed to go potty, wash my face and eat dinner with everyone else. As I asked what happened through my tears, she took my hand, picked up my bag and led me back down that long hallway through those double doors. I can still hear them close behind me. I had a sick feeling and knew my mom was not coming, but as a small child, I still had eternal hope that I was not going to be disappointed again.

I had to unpack my bag, put everything away, put the day's clothes in the hamper; put my nightgown on and brush my teeth. We also had to say our prayers every night. I am not proud of this but it is one of my first memories of telling a lie. The weekend dorm mom asked if I said my prayers. Holding back my tears I told her I did. I could not make myself say any prayer. I was struggling with the question of whether there was a God and if so, was He mean?

If this were a test, my mom failed miserably. The last part of my stay was a blur full of pain, isolation and loneliness.

I remember on this night, Rebecca, a little girl from the adjoining room, with the biggest brown eyes and a pixie cut, snuck into my room. Rebecca whispered to me she was sorry that my mom did not come. Rebecca said they told the other children I might be sad tonight but they were told not to talk to me about it. Rebecca risked Ms. Rita's wrath and demerits by sneaking into my room after lights out. She tried to make me feel better sharing that she did not have a mom at all. Hers went to Heaven. That was of little comfort; I still wanted my mom and really did not know where Heaven was.

Ms. Rita had another face. I saw it when I was awarded my consolation prize the very next weekend. Ms. Rita advised me, "This is the one and only time this is gonna happen for you." I was directed to pack up again, escorted back through those double doors. She made it clear my parents were not coming. I watched as my arch-nemesis turned into something that sounded sugary sweet. She even squeezed my shoulder saying to the couple that I had a hard week. The couple it turns out was taking me for a weekend visit. I listened as she chatted and spoke with these people I did not know. I watched Ms. Rita and wondered, "Who is this strange person and why is she sending me with these other people?" I wondered if my mom went to heaven too, like Rebecca's.

They were kind to me. I was given candy and chips. I sat by their fireplace, listening to them talking. The lady said to the man, "She's so quiet and well behaved, I don't understand why they call her a rebel." Apparently, they too, had been warned to be careful where they took me and even at my tender age I was labeled a flight risk or a runner. I guess they were referring to the time I tried to get out of a moving car. That attempt was to get to my brother. All the flight risk stuff, I was not sure what that meant. I had never been on a plane in my life.

That visit was nice but short-lived. I felt like a library book, checked out and checked right back in again. What was weird too, was that Ms. Rita looked almost happy to see me.

A word on the two faces of Ms. Rita: within the next week, Ms. Rita heard I was talking about having abilities to see and know things. I explained that to another little girl on the swing set from my perspective as an eight-year old child. I told that girl I knew she was telling the truth about being hurt and I told her why I knew. I described her mother's boyfriend. I knew what he did.

Well, I was called into Ms. Rita's living quarters to be questioned about it with much older girls witnessing. I told her the truth on the matter. Ms. Rita did not like my truth. Her response to my truth was to smack me open-handed on my face. This was hard enough to knock me back, but I did not fall down. This hurt so bad. She inquired again, "I'm gonna ask you one more time." Guess what? I answered again, truthfully. She came at me with a wide berth, full on, striking my face, causing my nose to bleed. She was seething, calling me a liar, asking me how I knew that.

What I had confirmed was contained in a closed file. I did not deviate from what I knew to be the truth. All the while she was telling me not to bleed on her rug. She wanted to make sure my nose was not broken and did eventually shove a towel in my face to stop the bleeding.

Ms. Rita did not send me to school the next day. Nobody saw me. She had food brought in to me. She told me I was sick with a fever and needed to stay in my room. I was not, but my face sure did hurt. Now, I ask you, who is the liar?

**Here is what I know now:**

I was thinking about forgiveness and the nature of it. We have to muster up genuine compassion for those who have wronged us instead of allowing anger toward them to eat at us. People would say, give it time. All time does is give you a way to accommodate grief; like a sudden and permanent limp it does not stop you completely, but it will forever alter the way you move through the world.

We should not stay stuck in the past. We learn by trial and error. We all misjudge. We will look for anything to make the hurt stop. It can be a gut-wrenching experience. If you continue this way, your power lays dying. If you could release them, you would know more peace.

It is tough to let go of resentments. If you are going to pursue revenge, you better dig two graves because the hatred in your heart will destroy you. Forgiveness does not happen quickly.

If I am to be a being of love, that means love is all I have inside of me. Forgiveness is a mighty big word. It is still a work in progress.

So many hurdles. I can jump them all, maybe with a little pain from the highest of jumps.

# Chapter Twelve
## Order from Chaos

I felt lost
Somewhere between midnight
And a hurricane
Each second might be hard
To chew
Each minute might be tough
To swallow

## Order from Chaos

Back in the 90s as an adult, I returned to walk through, a term I am going to use loosely, the children's "home." At that time, it was still used to house children. I was contemplating that I would one day share my story. I had been asked more than once by more than one person. After walking the halls of that place for what was the final time, I realized then and there that I could not verbalize what I was thinking and feeling, much less commit it to paper. It was too painful.

What I did do was take any notes, recordings and anything I could find that would keep the bandages on old wounds from being torn off to be locked away and used for a different time and place.

Three words to describe the building: austere, cold and steely. I brought a friend for support who recognized my description from the past, saying softly, "Nothing has changed." The wallpaper, paint, bedspreads, the grand piano; all sickeningly familiar. Time stood still, including the raw grip of gut wrenching sadness that washed over me.

The man who escorted me through the building knew the reason for my visit. I did not know what to make of the man; he asked me several times, "How are you doing?" He was curious about me. He knew it must have been a visceral experience. The place was more than I could handle. I left at one point, long enough to go outside for air and threw up. I did not recall that; it was relayed to me years later.

Going through the building that night, I once again heard the double doors close. I felt the anxiety rise from my chest into my throat and voices whispered in the hallway from my past, reminding me there was no order from chaos. The only redeeming factor was I knew I could leave. I could reach into my pocket for the comfort of my car keys.

Every click of my heels on those floors was a sad reminder of trust broken. If I could not trust kids nor adults, then who? I was closed off; I was not ready. This story had to wait. With age comes wisdom, then stories and strength. I knew one day I would share it all. It was not time yet.

I knew one of the most dangerous roads for me to go down was the "what ifs."

The irony of the building itself was that it housed lonely children and their spirits died in that process. In 2017, I wanted to try to visit again. I learned the building was no longer a Children's Home, but surprisingly it housed hospice patients who went there so they would not die alone. I thought, "Shouldn't I be over this by now?" Nothing that has ever happened there has lost its sting. I would never be able to close that chapter.

Once upon a time, they killed children's spirits there. The irony was now even adults go there to die so they are not alone. Death really does not take a vacation and I think this terrible paradox is one of life's greatest mysteries. Life for me is not the same, but the building has never lost its meaning.

In terms of death, it could mean people, places or things you leave behind. God took care of this for me. Time had passed, the door was closed. I let it go.

**Here is what I know now:**

Is there order from chaos?

No one is rallying around you with the same enthusiasm as with the pain and criticism they brought. Then the day comes when the risk to remain silent and keep your pain buried is more painful than the risk to acknowledge it and find your strength.

For those who authentically love me and that I love, in their defense, when I am down, I do not usually like an audience. I have been known to clear a room with just a look.

There is a first time for everything. Your heart gets broken. It is time for a pity party. I get my ten minutes like everyone else. It takes courage to turn inward, to dissect what you are feeling and to recognize your pain, whatever that may be.

We cannot hold onto the past. The best thing we can do is pray that we break our hearts wide open so that love for the whole world falls in.

The cool thing about learning how to overcome your fear and negative emotion is that you have to be willing to choose love and let go of resentment. It is hard to face the truth and realize that your whole life is a series of choices made by you, not to you. You are not a victim. Victim does not look pretty on anybody.

When we can finally obtain the gift of each situation, we are indeed living a peace-filled and blessed life.

# Chapter Thirteen
## Trifecta Mess

Sorrow and joy exist side by side.
Both are true and both are real.
Wisdom is making the space to hold
two opposing truths at the same time.
Memories are the unending circle.

## Trifecta Mess

Apparently, for whatever reason, there was no transitioning from the orphanage to home. After three years, I went back to that small little house full of noise, chaos and dysfunction at its finest. It was the trifecta of all messes. It was not Walton's Mountain.

My siblings and I were unceremoniously reunited that summer. It turns out my aunt and uncle were in town with their two children. I think they showed up due to the bomb I dropped.

My mom seemed to be healthy and well to me. Maybe that's one of those fantasies a small child has to cling to and hope lives eternal. She told me, "You and Jayne are going to be spending some time with Aunt Nina* and Uncle Adolph*." Horrified, I could not bear the thought of going. My mom announced we were going there to visit. It turned out, my mom was not doing that well. Jayne and I were to go there for the summer. The idea of sleepovers with my younger sister to protect made me nauseous. I had a secret.

I did what children sometimes have to do. I first begged and cried not to go. I disclosed to my mom that not only did he scare me, but Uncle Adolf had touched me. I told my mom that he touched me in my private place and disclosed this fact to save Jayne and prevent the visit to their home. Well, what do you know? My mom called my grandma. She called the police. She told my stepdad. I struck the match that hit the detonator. Boom! There was an explosion.

My mom believed me in those moments. Reality quickly came crashing down on her too. My stepfather's reaction to my mother was, "I can't wait until natural selection weeds out whatever part of your brain made you like this. You didn't question her?" What my mother understood was that she was dependent and fearful of where that would take her this time next year.

Anger is a great catalyst, but a terrible life companion. She had no choice but endure his wrath, sit back and "let him handle it" when he came home from work. He was angry, knowing the police had been called. He might not be able to keep my secret. There would be embarrassment and uninvited trouble.

The police came. They took me away from the house. My stepdad protested. I picked at a hamburger while the detective asked me questions. He was clear that I was not in trouble. The detective later told my mom and stepdad how much detail I provided and that he believed me. His years of experience led him to know I had been hurt. My family told the detective that I was always making up stories, my stepdad in particular. He told the detective that he would get to the bottom of this. I was left with my family.

My mom spoke to other family members who proclaimed, "She's gonna ruin the family!" My stepdad called me pathological and told me I would burn in hell. He produced a Bible. He drank, made me swear on it, drank some more and so it went. He kept saying, "Let's try this again." He worked on me that entire evening to make me take it back, to recant my statement.

The phone rang all night. Aunt Nina called, tearfully asking how would she feed her children if I did not quit telling stories? I was told later Uncle Adolf's response was, "I didn't do it, and if I had, we're talking about a little stink finger, nothing major. She's her mother's daughter."

I was tired and hungry. I did not want to go to hell, but my stepdad made the orphanage look good. I thought for sure I would be given a one-way ticket back there.

Joey jumped on the crazy train and took a little piece of my heart with him. He went along with them and encouraged me to lie about my truth. He believed me but said, "All you have to do is tell them you made it up." I guess Joey was done with the bombs exploding too.

Our families are our first connection. When we are kids, we are taught to stay away from a hot stove at all costs. We are hardwired to avoid pain, to get away from painful stimuli. The reaction is primitive. We do the same thing with emotional trauma. After hours of enduring psychological torture, at the hands of stepdad, I took my hands off the stove.

The man used tactics such as promising to love me if I would just tell the truth. I was worried about burning in hell, only one among the many other things he threatened during that long, treacherous night. To stop it all, to fix it, I took back my truth, recanted.

The next morning, I was paraded out in front of the detective, stared at the floor and I did lie. I never looked up. I felt real terror as I looked at my stepdad. There was no end to my misery. He even threatened to send me to my Uncle Adolf's house anyway. He made sure to drive home the idea that the family was not happy with me for lying.

The ordeal all began because I believed I could trust my mother. After all, she was one person I was closest to on this earth, my first connection. My relationship with my mother was intricate and unyielding before this day. After this day and up to the day of her death, the relationship with my mother remained complicated at best.

As it were, the cavalry (Aunt June* and Uncle Jake*) came riding in with an RV and it was decided that Jayne and I would go with them and their two daughters on a trip to California and Arizona. My aunt and uncle never spoke of any family things, at least not to us. But I had a feeling that my Aunt June had little patience with my stepfather.

It was an epic summer. They tried to make sure we had a good trip. We saw the Painted Desert, the Petrified Forest and stood at the Grand Canyon. I learned to love cream cheese and cucumber sandwiches. I swam in Lake Havasu. They were building the London Bridge that summer. It was the first time I felt the warm breeze of Palm Springs on my face. I dreamt of tacos for years after that summer and loved Mexican food. I had no idea what an Officer's Club was, but we got to go there a lot. They treated my Uncle Jake funny when we went there, and I did not understand why because after all, he was the same man who had jumped in the pool and played with us on those hot summer afternoons. He became a full bird Colonel and flew jets.

My Uncle Adolf was an evil child predator, as was at least one cousin in particular.

See that you do not despise one of these little ones.
For I tell you that in heaven their angels
always see the face of my Father who is in heaven.

~Matthew 18:10~

In this Bible verse, Jesus is speaking about the children and those who would offend or violate one of them. Those who violate a child would be in serious trouble with the Father in heaven because He sees everything that happens. God does not like ugly.

There is a special place in hell for those that would harm any child for any reason.

**Here is what I know now:**

I cannot change what is and what was.

In a perfect world, my recommendation would be to handle your memories with care. This last year for me felt as though I had been at a permanent crossroads, as a lot of my life has been - somewhere between midnight and a hurricane.

It has been a crazy time of transition for me and for so many others I know. In the beginning, for me, after the numbness wore off following my mother's death, I felt transported to a time and a place from my childhood. I felt as though I had lost my courage, conviction and confidence. I found myself stuck there and unsure about everything, unable to make any decision of importance. Broken.

My mother was a woman with whom I had a very complicated relationship. Nonetheless, she was my mother. I loved her.

This last year has led me on a journey that has been an overwhelming process of sifting and sorting the good and the bad memories. The complex childhood memories and the complicated adult realities. I am forced to remember she was flawed but also know she was capable of kindness and love as we all can be.

My prayer before the second-year anniversary rolls around is to not whitewash the reality of my life or hers. I have never wanted to be the daughter who repeats the sins of the mother through blind reverence and even more blinding tears for a lost childhood and my lost loved ones. It has left scars and deep wounds that have left me with the arduous task of trying to heal. Her death opened doors and brought home the reality of chapters I had long since closed.

A full year has passed. Death has shown me it is uncomfortable. For those mourning, there are those people that show up and the ones that do not. In addition to everything else, you have to process. One single death brings about what experts would term as secondary losses, the heartbreakers. They take the shape of the people who cannot turn and face you in the depth of your pain and the monumental life change that has just happened to you. They could not possibly understand the history nor do they want to. The only thing people get is what affects them.

There is a before and an after. My struggle has been not to continue to get lost in the what ifs. It is a work in progress.

Death is also the memories you leave behind. Of course, I never wanted my mother to die. I would give my arms, legs and a multitude of other appendages to change my past and what her destiny became.

What I have learned about myself in the months after her death, I would not trade to bring her back. What I have found out is healing does not come when the days get better.

You cannot control memories by disposing of them or deliberately seeking them out. What I have learned is I have to maintain a balance of what I hold onto and what I let go of, and time will heal the rest. I will never have all of the answers to every question. At least, not here. Everyone will have their truth, but this truth is mine.

# Chapter Fourteen
## Turbulence Ahead

Overthinking creates worry
and then fun goes to die.

## Turbulence Ahead

Jayne and I took our first plane ride back home from California to St. Louis. It was my understanding my aunt made my stepdad pay for airplane tickets back. There was a huge family fight. Apparently, that was my fault too. He could not drink because he had to pick us up at the airport. He was angry.

Everything set him off; he would explode without warning. For example, I had not ironed correctly, so my stepdad grabbed me by my throat and held me above his head in the corner of the tiny room with my feet dangling. He was choking me; this only took one of his hands. I could not breathe. Joey came in and was punching him to get him drop me, Joey screaming, "You're hurting her!" My stepdad dropped me. I fell into a crumpled, bruised pile on the floor.

After a glimpse into what seemed a normal and stable summer, returning to this existence was more than I could bear. I wanted to die. I thought to be dead would be better and my only way to escape. Immediately after dropping to the floor, I went and grabbed my mother's newly filled prescription and swallowed all of them.

Joey saw me swallow the full bottle and told my mom. My stepdad did not believe me, but my mom called my grandparents who drove over with another aunt, Hilda*, to pick me up and they took me to the hospital. The hospital pumped my stomach after giving me this black charcoal mixture that made me throw up. Warning: I would never recommend this. If you ever feel this desperate, there is always someone out there to help.

My grandparents and Aunt Hilda took me home. My grandmother, fearing I was still in harm's way, made her own concoction for me to drink consisting of raw eggs, castor oil and milk. She wanted to make sure I was not going to die.

It turned out Aunt Hilda was living with my grandparents after a divorce. Uncle Adolph and Aunt Nina moved out of the home my grandparents owned. My aunt and uncle were not known for keeping up with their bills, so they relocated.

My stepdad said I would never amount to anything. I was not prepared for the pain of coming home. Time could not fix everything. One summer in the grand scheme of things could not erase the chaos in that house that swirled around my entire family. My strength was depleted, and I hit an all-time low at the tender age of twelve. I did not know how to give myself time to be sad, frustrated or even angry. I did not know how to heal. I had not learned to, nor was I equipped to climb out yet. I had no idea how to preempt darkness. By then, I journaled a lot. That was helpful. Much later in my life, I started a poem and finished it in this last couple of years.

It began with:

If I could stand and take my place, where would that be? I searched my mind. I searched my soul. Where would I find me?

I defied the odds and the statistics and was not known for self-medicating in any of its forms. I knew there had to be a better way for me. I did not know what that would be or how it could ever happen.

Having knowledge and possessing wisdom are two very different things. The best people to spend time with offer feedback. I needed support, quiet stabilizers.

Which brings me back to Aunt Hilda. She was a quiet stabilizer, for a few minutes. She taught me some life lessons, such as, "I was good enough." She believed I was not beyond repair. She took me to top-notch restaurants, showed me which forks to use and how to set a table. Aunt Hilda was the type of woman who believed that if I did not use a word correctly in a sentence, I should grab a dictionary and read it to her. She encouraged me on the one hand but she was also certifiably crazy on the other.

The problem with that was she wanted to exorcise demons from me. So out came another Bible. This Bible was used in a different way, but still scary. She took me to church and told the congregation, "This child has strange dreams and makes predictions!"

She taught me how to dress, how to walk into any room knowing I was as good as anyone else. I had decent clothes to wear and could finally hold my head up with pride. However, she also wanted to perform an exorcism on me. She was like a total solar eclipse on steroids. She was a conundrum. Aunt Hilda kept me on my toes but now for different reasons.

Aunt Hilda believed having a soft heart in a cruel world was not weakness, it was courage.

**Here is what I know now:**

Do not get trapped. The verb, "stuck" means trapped into something. Stuck on stupid is an adjective, a prolonged state of being completely clueless when someone just does not get it; a person who does not know better. When we know better, we do better. We all have been guilty of doing foolish things.

Some people are broken and they get mad at you for being whole.

My attitude is to keep your negativity to yourself. After I have watched people poison their own lives, I would be silly to let them do the same to mine. Try to be positive and give people like this the benefit of the doubt which is an excellent tactic for not allowing them to get to you. Remind yourself they are not all bad.

The hardest thing you will have to do is keep your emotions in check. Clueless people are professionals at making other people upset or enraged. If you want to come out of any conversation or interaction stress-free, you have to keep your cool. Acknowledge strengths of an individual who is acting sophomoric.

At the beginning of our adulthood, we do many things wrong. You do things that do not work, and you may screw up royally. You pay your dues. Suddenly, after all of the years of toiling, you have a grand epiphany; this is what we believe would happen with all of us. We figure out the right path.

People who get stuck and remain there are waiting for the world to present opportunities. It is not the action that leads to success; it is the action of seeking solutions and staying in control of your emotions and feelings. Take responsibility for yourself.

I have always said, "We all make errors. Mistakes are what we choose not to correct." We need to learn to focus on the good relationships and the good parts of our lives. Multiply them.

## WHEN SLEEP WON'T COME

If I could drown my sorrow
And you could carry my pain
How often could you do it
When it makes no sense
Nor can it be changed

I sit quietly
Tears falling inside
Not often out
Feelings are real and legitimate

I hold myself up
When the sun shines brightly
And we are all awake
I can manage these painful
Moments

When the sun goes down
And it is time to rest
You close your eyes and
Do your best

Are we not hardwired to
Avoid pain
We don't dare
Let others see

So you are awake in the darkness
When others do sleep
Counting those tears instead
Of those sheep

Let not your heart be troubled
Hand it over to someone
Bigger than you

Or sleep will elude you
And you will never know
What to do

Relax
Picture the calm
Turn your mind off
Or soon it will be dawn

# Chapter Fifteen

## Well, We Were All Born to Die

## Decathect

Sometimes we don't want to go
where we are headed.
It takes a death to get us there.

## Well, We Were All Born to Die
## Decathect

According to Freud, bereavement was not complete until the mourner was able to withdraw emotional attachment from the deceased (decathect*) and reinvest that emotional energy into a new relationship or, at least, back into life.

Starting from 1972, at the age of thirteen I was indoctrinated and found myself staring death straight in the face.

It was early March of 1972. I left as usual that day to catch the bus for school. It was unusually warm. My normal routine before leaving the house for school was to give my grandparents both a hug and a kiss. Something made me turn around and give my grandfather a second kiss. We would always say see you later, not goodbye. Unfortunately, it was goodbye to my grandpa.

I was in Home Economics class when over the loudspeaker, I was asked to be sent to the office immediately. At this point in my life, it was unusual because it was not my heart's desire to get in trouble of any kind. I told my teacher I did not want to go because my grandpa is dead. She said to me, "That is ridiculous. What an imagination you have."

My first stop was to the nearest toilet, and I promptly threw up. Then I headed into the office to meet with the principal. He told me Aunt Hilda was waiting for me at the crosswalk. Out of the building we went. She stood there waiting stoically as the principal walked me to her. Somehow, I knew this was not going to end well.

The hospital where my grandpa was taken was located directly across the street from my school. Aunt Hilda told me Grandpa was sick and I needed to come with her. As we were walking into the tiny private room where my grandma was waiting and crying, Aunt Hilda was telling me they were still working on Grandpa. I did not want to tell her he was dead because I was afraid of her. I did not need an exorcism performed on me at that moment or any other time in my life. Aunt Hilda was crazy scary, and I never knew when she would pull that Bible out of her handbag.

My grandma explained what happened. She called Aunt Hilda and told her that Grandpa had called out from the bathroom because he needed his overalls pulled up. Grandma had already called for an ambulance. She needed to get his overalls pulled up because she did not want him to go to the hospital like that. He was heavy. Grandma knew he was gone before they ever took him to the hospital and had arrived DOA (dead on arrival).

A doctor came into the tiny room and told us that my grandpa had an aortic aneurysm. He was probably gone before he ever left his home.

I want to clear up family lore. No one, other than Aunt Hilda, my grandmother and myself had been anywhere near my grandfather on the day he died or days before. There were no deathbed discussions.

Before we had the funeral, we had to wait for family members to come from out of town. At the funeral home, as most of you will know, there was family drama. People showed up crying like crazy after several years of never visiting or speaking to my grandpa. I did not understand. It was World War III. I found it disgusting! However, I was too young to have a voice with what I knew to be the truth.

Aunt Hilda did ask me the question at the funeral, "How did you know your grandfather was dead?" The principal mentioned it to her. She said, "We will talk about this later."

I wanted to disappear.

The house was silent for some time. My grandmother did not want to work things out with the disruptive and now estranged family members from my grandfather's funeral, in part, because she was growing older and now dependent on my Aunt Hilda. Aunt Hilda was not having it. However, they showed back up at my brother's funeral only fourteen months later.

Joey was fifteen years old at the time of his death. I was fourteen; however, I remember as if it were yesterday. Joey did not have a license, just a permit to drive. He was given the keys to the vehicle he should not have been driving. It belonged to our stepfather.

A drunk driver struck Joey and left the scene of the accident. It was tragic and unnecessary. Joey survived for six days after the collision in an ICU on a respirator. There was no hope. He was 31 days shy of his sixteenth birthday.

Joey's accident happened on what was then a highway known as 244. A man crossed over the grassy median and struck Joey who at that age, did not have the skill set to maneuver around that vehicle coming at him. Joey's vehicle flipped over, he went through the windshield and was thrown from the car. Years later, that same drunk driver that hit my brother was responsible for killing a family of four.

My brother was a fifteen-year-old kid that did not know any better. He was forced, like me, to grow up quickly. Joey would not have thought anything about giving himself a driving lesson. Driving without a license is not punishable by death.

The wake and funeral lasted for three days. Young and old packed the building. The fire marshal showed up and made people form a line that wrapped around the building. They kept coming.

The family drama ensued at Joey's funeral, too. Thank goodness the fire marshal was there because he diffused the situation. They were not pleased to be told they had to stand in line with everyone else.

Joey was my rock. I was devastated and did not know how I was going to go on without him. We promised we would always be there for each other.

In Joey's high school yearbook, they listed a dedication to him. He was well liked and missed by all.

It took me over a year to function after Joey's death. The worst of the deaths, not that one can measure, was yet to come.

**Here is what I know now:**

There is something horribly wrong when the death of a young person occurs who has so much more of a road left on their journey.

I have been thinking a lot about how the shifts in paradigms from old to young will continue to occur through the duration of our lives. It is so sad, and the big question is why? Shock and immeasurable pain are real for the loved ones left behind. They are trying to make sense of the unspeakable grief.

It is impossible to understand or begin to act as if you do understand. The easy platitudes such as, "God has gained another angel" or "It is part of God's plan" are awkward and uncomfortable even if you believe it. It feels like a test you did not study for, and you are not going to pass.

Sometimes it is better to say nothing than try to fix it (I did not say avoid it). Just listen.

The difference between a young person dying and a much older person dying feels like an insult and somewhat of a cruel joke.

When a young person dies, what the family wants to hear is: "It sucks, and I hate you have to go through this. I am here for you, and I will still be here for you if you want to cry or when you are angry. If you need to yell about it, I am here. I will still be here if you want to laugh. I may not understand what you are going through, but I will still be here days and years from now."

With that in mind, there are no perfect words, no silver lining or light at the end of the tunnel. What they would be thinking, "I don't care what the plan is, I don't like this plan, and it would be better if they were here with me." I would agree with this.

I never thought I would be thinking about this much death, how and why we deal with it the way we do. I certainly do not have all of the answers.

For those out there grieving today, it does suck! I am thinking and praying for all of you and realize it is a long and arduous journey.

# Chapter Sixteen
## I Am Perfectly Flawed

I want to scream out loud.
I am trapped in a time warp.
I really cannot navigate.
At least, not now.

It is difficult to retrieve
people and things
lost back in a faraway land stolen
by minutes, days and years.

In the end, we all become stories.

## I Am Perfectly Flawed

The year was 1974. I became a mother for the first time. I was a teenage mom. I wanted to build a connection and focus on trust, not tricks. That is how you earn respect. Trust is fragile and mistrust is self-fulfilling. The odds were against me and the deck was stacked. There are two kinds of pain: pain that hurts you and pain that changes you.

This book is the first of three. I wish I could say I did not suffer any more losses, a prince rode up on a white horse and I lived happily ever after. The truth is, that is not my story. The father of my children was not like wine and cheese. He did not get better with age. I divorced that guy after seven years. But later, I did find my prince and love of my life. He has stood by my side for just about thirty years. But more on that later.

I suffered the death of a child. I suffered miscarriages. So much loss. But, for whatever reason, God saw it fit to give me two beautiful sons. I was ill-equipped with no real tools and no one to mentor me. I was blessed with plenty of judges and probably PTSD (post-traumatic stress disorder). What I knew I could not do was have an abortion or adoption. For me, these were not options. I thought it was going to make me a Godly woman. All it made me was a teenage mom.

I thought if I finished my education and worked hard, one day my grown sons would recognize it for what it was and realize I loved them with my whole heart. I fought the demons of my past and people every step of the way. The ones who were drilling holes in my boat when I was not looking.

We all have our life lessons, and I received mine. I have to move on from what hurt me. No pain comes without a purpose, but I will never forget what it taught me. Every great success requires struggle. There were things I missed and should have been present for, which left my sons disappointed and hurt.

I can say things get jaded and iced over with stories, but winter thaws and spring comes. I could sit here, reinvent the wheel and write about the Rubik's cube but I put it down for awhile because turning it and turning it adds to the confusion.

I have spent most of my life trying to heal the broken places. My sons both have terrific educations that are higher than mine. I like to think that was due to my encouragement and support every step of the way.

Just because you are struggling, does not mean you are failing. I did not want to be the voice in my sons' heads haunting them as my mother was for me. I may have fallen short a time or two. Get a room full of mothers together and ask them if they got it right every time, all of the time. We all want to be Facebook fabulous, but we are not. We are human beings, flaws and all.

I would have loved to have been a thirty-year-old mother with a loving husband by my side. I was fifteen when I got pregnant. Scientists say the adult brain reaches full maturity at the age of twenty-five or so. The fact my sons are still standing is a miracle in itself. I thank God every day and hope at the end of my life they can forgive me for my worst decisions and unchecked emotions, and realize how much I did sacrifice. I would lay down and die for either one of my boys who are now grown men.

As a Grandmother, I have a chance to do it better. Maybe not immediately but eventually.

Never forget you have a chance. Know your worth.

During my entire childhood, as I look back on it now, it was the lesson in playing it safe. When I became a full-grown adult, I had to step out of my comfort zone so that people would no longer doubt what I said much less believe I have a gift. I am a person, a woman and I am perfectly flawed.

Courage is not a lack of fear but the ability to act while facing fear. God will decide what we need. If it were left up to me, a mere human, I would seek revenge for all of us getting old. Instead, I have to look in the mirror and stand helplessly watching crow's feet creep up and counting grey hairs. I am thankful.

As I have been finishing writing this book, I feel like a phoenix rising from the fire. What I realized: God does not call the qualified, he qualifies the called.

I had been forced to go back in time and remember watching my mother's life play out and her mother's life before her, whether they knew it or not. They both have been with God for some time.

There is no way over the fire. There is no way around it. You have to walk straight through it. For me, that is what I am doing. I get to decide what I need. My mother and her mother did not. They gave me the realization of, "Do it afraid." It was years in the making.

I have come to realize I have three different ways of handling things. Sometimes I want to talk through it. Sometimes I want to get my mind off of it for awhile. Sometimes, I just want to be alone, and I write. There is nothing wrong with stepping back before you walk through the fire.

More than we are doers, we are deciders. Once the decisions are made, the doing is effortless. Death taught me:  there will be times when all you have is your fire.

**Here is what I know now:**

What happens when your life gets turned upside down?

To turn upside down, when used figuratively, usually means to disorganize or to put in disarray. Nothing is the way it used to be. It is about to change but often shocking and upsetting. It does not have to be negative. Tell that to someone who is walking through the fire. They have been betrayed and just took a gut punch from someone they have trusted. They are still reeling from the first blow, and another one gets thrown. The pain is intense.

What is a betrayal and why is this one of the most devastating losses? There are purposeful aspects of deception. It is an unfortunate characteristic of human nature.

The traitors are the most devastating kind because it did not have to occur. It occurs because of someone's deliberate hurtful behavior, carelessness or their weakness. Unlike a loss such as death or illness, there is usually some choice involved.

When someone you trust lies to you, cheats on you, abuses you or hurts you by putting their self-interest first, that is the worst kind of betrayal. You go through denial, shock and are numb. This stage is usually relatively short. Then rage sets in because you fully acknowledge what has happened and there is intense anger. You vent your emotions, and it escalates. Sadness occurs.

I believe it is best to talk to a trusted or unbiased friend or an expert. Finally, we accept and deal with it, begin to heal and then move on. Recovering is difficult.

What to do with a traitor? What should our response be? How do we keep the pain from robbing us of our ability to love, much less trust? Is there a smart way to deal with it? I would rather be a fool fifty times over than fatally wrong once.

I am not saying it is easy. You are not going to be able to stop running the story in your head. However, you will get to a place in time and mean it when you say, “I forgive you,” to those who betrayed you. Forgiveness is the gift you give yourself. Looking in the mirror and knowing your own self-worth is another. You can only do this after you let yourself off the hook.

# Chapter Seventeen
## Broken Crayons Still Color

The great skill in life is learning to compromise.
Do not be willing to concede.
The concession is accepting it,
And there is no strength of character there.

Accepting it is when you know you are
Allergic to Kool-Aid and you drink it anyway.

Decide to stay away from negative conversation.
It is a downward spiral unless there is a positive solution.

## Broken Crayons Still Color

It is better to cross the line and suffer consequences than stare at the line for the rest of your life. It was time for a conversation. I felt nauseous.

Broken crayons still color but not when it is time to go to hospice. For the one-hundredth time, my mother was transported to the hospital like it had a revolving door. She was not going to recover. I wanted her to go to Heaven with her dignity. I needed this for her. I wanted Daryl to agree with me to give this last gift of love to our mother. Mom wanted to go home.

We are all broken. There will be times in your life when all of your instincts tell you to do something that defies logic, upsets your plans and may even seem crazy to others.

I said a prayer, texted my little brother and made it clear we needed to talk. I was not angry but was hurting for him, for me but mainly for Mom; suffering upon suffering. I knew the struggle was real but so is God.

We are all good lawyers for our mistakes but good judges for the mistakes of others. One of the hardest things in life is to let go of what you thought was real.

Not caring what other people think is the best choice you will ever make. Plan your future with purpose. Remember that your mind will affect your mouth. So, if you want to get over a problem, stop talking about it. Put it in writing.

My prayer was, "Hi God, it is me again. I know You are listening. Do You have an army available? I am not asking for me, but for my mom. She needs Your help. I know Your job is to love the fallen, restore the broken and be a part of the healing, not hurting. Mom wants to come home. Can we have this gift for her?"

I knew the time was short when I texted my little brother. I prayed to God Daryl would hear me. We had a truthful, honest conversation. My heart was breaking for both of us. Daryl needed to listen with his heart, not his ears. It crushed me, but it was a conversation we needed to have.

My mother began her journey home "for real" on November 30. We had an opportunity, as a family, to come together while she was in short-term hospice. On December 9, 2016, my mom went home to meet her Lord and Savior. We know we will see her again.

What kept me going in those days before her death? My beliefs and pure adrenaline. I sat there on and off for those many days, some much longer than others. On one particular day, as I was watching others' tears fall, listening to my mother's breathing, and feeling numb, I began to write. Behind every trial and sorrow we have to shoulder, God had a purpose. Why were we sitting here like this keeping a vigil? God has a purpose. People needed to say goodbye.

Change does not come if we wait for some other person or a different time. Some people believe that holding on and hanging in there are signs of strength. However, there are times in our lives when it takes much more courage to know when to let go and then do it.

"God is always in control. Last night the earth spun off its axis." As a result, Mom was going to gain entry into Heaven. She was going home. When we are on our knees and feel there is no hope, that is when God does His best work.

When you are stricken and cannot bear it any longer, every path leads home. Every step is birth. Every step is death. Every step is toward home. Home is within you.

Heaven knows we should never be ashamed of our tears. They are the rain that washes away the blinding dust of the earth.

I do not know what they are called, the spaces between the seconds. Despite all, never stop looking for happiness, peace and home. We are all looking for home.

I asked my mom to save a seat at the table. We all did.

**Here is what I know now:**

Birth, life, death. What are we doing in between the first and the last of these three things?

In these last years, being over 55 has ushered in an exciting era of death positivity. There are more and more opportunities to consider your own death and plan for it. I am even receiving mail from local funeral homes to preplan everything as if I am ordering off of a menu at my favorite restaurant.

People who think and talk about death are often labeled morbid or death-obsessed. Talk about your demise and funeral wishes to your friends and family. Most of them will not want to. It is the quickest way to clear a room.

It sounds dark. We are all going to die but hopefully not too soon or too horribly. While we are waiting, every day is a new opportunity to work on us. To do something positive for someone around you who does not expect it.

One of the downsides to being a conscious human is the awareness that someday you will die. Denial is the default in modern western culture.

I am hoping mine is years away, but I live every day as if it could be tomorrow, tonight or an hour from now. At least, I am trying to. My mother's death has taught me so much about my own mortality. In particular, what I do not want.

We are what our thoughts have made us. Yes, we are all going to die. The honest truth is having balance in all things can be a source of real happiness. My concern is what I am doing in the middle, in the time between my birth and death. We need to concern ourselves with the present. God has given us no control over the moments following.

I want to spend the rest of my life laughing, not buried under a to-do list, much less making my funeral arrangements. I did that some time ago. However, I do appreciate the options provided by those in the funeral industry. So many choices!

# Epilogue

You cannot change the past, but you can take responsibility for how you handle yourself moving forward. There are times we are forced to do it afraid.

You have to start taking care of yourself. You are loved. You are not defined as a failure because other people believe it to be true. For me, it is not "The End" of my story.

There are dreams beyond all of this pain. Let go of what should be. Dare to imagine creating a full and beautiful life for yourself. It takes baby steps. You have only but to look up at the stars and celebrate the small victories. Even when we cannot see them, they are there.

My home gives me a sense of security and comfort. Leaving requires me to move out of my comfort zone. My family represents a safe place to rest and recharge. Home is where you can be yourself. It is not a structure; it is not brick or mortar but a place inside your heart, deep in your soul. It is reflective.

God will it, so be it. Believe it, and you will gain patience. Grief is not a gallon of milk or a carton of eggs. It is learning to reset your heart. Resetting your heart is letting go of the picture of the way you wanted it to be.

I wish I could tell you grief would end with a service on the calendar. What no one tells you is that death is the calendar. Some might think that there is an acceptable shelf life, a handful of weeks and then it should be off the shelf out of our home and permanently removed with the weekly trash service, if it were only that simple.

Grief is a long journey. It does not mean you cannot live a happy life, but it is a choice and takes work. Grief never really goes away. You get through each death. You never really get over it. I am going to give myself a break. I was left reeling with my mom's death. Up until now, I did not understand that when my mom took her last breath, I would be transported back in time to that four-year-old standing in the hallway saying, "Mommy don't leave me." It was like someone took a shovel and hit me in the face. I did not know how I was ever going to get back up again. Sometimes you are forced to revisit the past so you can finally lay it to rest. If that ever happens.

The key to grieving is not to try and stop it as quickly as possible. Grief cannot be shut off at will despite telling yourself otherwise. What matters is we acknowledge that we are in pain and try to find the goodness in our life despite it.

It is important to remember this: you did not ask to be born into a family with narcissistic people at the helm, but you have a chance every day to begin again, to get in touch with the beauty and the brilliance that is inside you. It has always been there. You deserve to feel wanted, respected and safe. It is your life. You get to call the shots. Remember that. You are more resilient than you know.

# Afterword

We are hard pressed on every side yet not crushed;
we are perplexed, but not in despair;
persecuted, but not forsaken;
struck down, but not destroyed.

~2 Corinthians 4:8-9~

Chin Up Buttercup. You have people that love you no matter what.

If you fall down one hundred times, I would encourage you to get on your knees and get back up the one hundred and first time. God has a plan.

After wrapping my brain around my life from 2014 to the end of 2017, I wanted to list the positives that came from the negatives.

1. If we think we got our life's lessons from early in life, God will call upon us again to demonstrate that we did.

2. My husband still loves me and we are still here. I am still breathing.

3. The sun is shining in Charlieville today.

4. My grandson is active, happy, loving and smart and I thank God for him daily!!!

5. I learned a new term called Doxing (identity theft on steroids). It is what authorities called it. It happened

to me, and I kept smiling and found humor in it. Nothing was fun about those eight weeks.

6. My mother began her journey home "for real" on November 30, 2016. We had the opportunity to, as a family, to come together for each other and my mother, while she was in short-term hospice.

7. On December 9, 2016, my mom went home to meet her Lord and Savior. We know we will see her again.

8. In between my mother's death and her service, a young man was going too fast on a service road, crossed over into my lane and hit me at 63+ mph head on. Stunned and somewhat hurt, I walked away. Protected! The same day, another woman had a head-on accident in the same place. She died.

9. On December 20, 2016, happy birthday to me, an hour before going to my mother's service, my sister-in-law received a phone call and was told that her dear, dear friend and family friend, Al, let go of his fight and he, too, headed home. She had family and friends present to support her.

10. My mother's service was not only beautiful, but you could feel the power of God in the building that day. I am grateful to my son and brother for being able to step up and do what they do best - teaching and music. I am thankful for all those who came together and helped.

11. What kept me going: my beliefs and pure adrenaline.

12. Christmas 2016 was surreal, happy, quiet and everything in between.

13. The key to grieving is not to try and stop it. What matters is we acknowledged we were in pain and tried to find the goodness in our lives despite it.

14. 2017 - the roller coaster continues...

15. The New Year in 2017 rolled in - yay! I learned how to deal with grief, and it does not have a shelf life. Mother Theresa said, "I am a pencil in the hand of God." I am finding this to be true. Thankfully God has our backs!

16. I am praying for a close friend and their family. They know who they are! She still has so much love and concern for my family.

17. On February 3, 2017, someone decided to go for a ride and crashed head on into my 100+-year-old walnut tree. The good news, the tree stopped him from hitting my house and harming anyone inside.

18. I am still trying to connect and reconnect with people. Thank God I have many patient friends and family. It has not been easy. However, when I look at my walnut tree, gouge and all, I know that God is good!

19. Why am I being protected? I may never know. There is still so much ahead, and I am truly grateful.

20. My husband and I could say, "give us a break" but God protected us from anything that was not sent by Him.

21. The fact anyone is reading this tells me there is much love in my life, friends and strangers alike.

22. Are some of these things inconvenient? Yes. As of 2018, will there be a second book in the works about this and so much more? Yes!

23. The story continues...

# Bibliography

- *Between Heaven and Earth: The Soul Purpose* (Alone at the Crossroads)
  ISBN: 0-9671280-0-5

- *The Mystical Side of Reality* (Audiocassette)
  ISBN: 0-9671280-1-3

- *Why Are We Here? (An Honest Truth)* (E-Book and CD)
  ISBN: 0-9671280-2-1

- *Destination Spirituality: A Guide Toward Inner Peace* (Paperback)
  ISBN: 0-9671280-8-0

- *Desperation, Fear and Love: The Great Motivators*
  ISBN: 0-9671280-6-4

- *Raw Emotion: When Time Stands Still* (E-Book and 2 CD Set)
  ISBN: 0-9671280-7-2

# Other Works by Joy M. Mills

(Including Bibliographic References)

## TELEVISION/RADIO APPEARANCES

- ABC KDNL 30 St. Louis The Allman Report
- CNN – America's Talking
- FX Breakfast Time
- CBS – The Gordon Elliott Show
- Aura Television (New York Cable)
- NBC – The Other Side
- ABC – Turning Point
- CNN – Talk Radio
- TLC – "Crossing Over" with John Edward
- Sirius Radio – The Laura Smith Show

## LECTURES/WORKSHOPS

- Band Wagon Promotions (People of Like Mind Expositions) (Illinois and Missouri)
- Psychics, Seers, and Mystics (New York and Canada)
- Whole Life and Whole Health Expositions (New York, California, Massachusetts, Illinois, Florida, and Georgia)
- Joy Mills Workshops (Missouri, New York, California, Florida, Ohio)
- Universal of Light Expos (Ohio)

## MEDIA PUBLICATIONS

- Articles about Joy Mills in Missouri/Illinois Newspapers
- Country magazine, the Hamptons, New York

- St. Louis magazine, August 1999
- St. Louis magazine, columnist, March 2001 through December 2003

BOOKS

- *Between Heaven and Earth: The Soul Purpose (Am I Good Enough?)*
  ISBN: 978-0-9671280-9-2

- *Between Heaven and Earth: The Soul Purpose (Alone at the Crossroads)*
  ISBN: 0-9671280-0-5

- *The Mystical Side of Reality* (Audiocassette)
  ISBN: 0-9671280-1-3

- *Why Are We Here? (An Honest Truth)* (Audiocassette)
  ISBN: 0-9671280-3-X

- *Why Are We Here? (An Honest Truth)* (E-Book and CD)
  ISBN: 0-9671280-2-1

- *Life, Death and Miracles* (E-Book and CD)
  ISBN: 0-9671280-4-8

- *Destination Spirituality: A Guide Toward Inner Peace* (Hardback)
  ISBN: 1-4010-7661-0

- *Destination Spirituality: A Guide Toward Inner Peace* (Paperback)
  ISBN: 0-9671280-8-0

- *Desperation, Fear and Love: The Great Motivators*
  ISBN: 0-9671280-6-4

- *Raw Emotion: When Time Stands Still* (E-Book and 2 CD Set)
  ISBN: 0-9671280-7-2

# Resources

Arch Phys Med Rehabil. Author manuscript; available in PMC 2015 Jul 27.
Published in final edited form as:
Arch Phys Med Rehabil. 2014 Jun; 95(6): 1223–1224.
doi: 10.1016/j.apmr.2013.06.002

Moody Bible Institute
820 N. LaSalle Street
Chicago, Illinois 60610

Long considered the gold standard of Bible-based education, Moody Bible Institute has been preparing students for ministry since 1886, with a combination of biblical knowledge and practical training.

St. Louis History Museum Archives
5700 Lindell Boulevard
St. Louis, Missouri 63112

Missouri Department of Social Services Children's Division
Main Office
205 Jefferson Street
Jefferson City, Missouri 65101

Chicago History Museum - Transportation
1601 N. Clark Street
Chicago, Illinois 60610

# What People Are Saying

"Joy is an amazing mentor, a woman of great courage, and a true friend. Through Joy, I have learned that sometimes things are not always as they seem, and that the answers to our questions will come in their own time if we pay attention to what is happening around us.

A woman with enormous courage to share her history, Joy has lived through many challenging situations in her lifetime, yet survived where others may have crumbled. Combined with her gift and the wisdom gained from each negative situation, she knows, and understands what others are going through and offers insights with compassion and empathy. In her readings, Joy tells what needs to be told without the sugar coating, but with refreshing and sometimes surprising observations. Joy calls it as she sees it, and serves it up with levity and humor where appropriate.

In this complicated and sometimes unforgiving world, I am grateful that Joy is here and offers wise counsel and hope where sometimes it seems things are hopeless."
~Pam P.

"Joy Mills told me about a path for my life and I didn't believe her. That was 25 years ago and sure enough, despite my best efforts, she nailed it. The best thing that came out of our talks? Our friendship. Her compassion, support, and insights are invaluable. Joy is so well respected in her field and yet few people know that her life has been a series of struggles that would break most people. And yet, her life is devoted to helping the rest of us see more clearly, and to be more kind and forgiving with each other."
~Helen M. T

"Joy and I have been with each other through the highs and lows of life from raising kids and grandkids to losing loved ones. I met her in a professional setting but I now know her personally and what is amazing about Joy is that no matter what happens in life, Joy's friendships, her faith, and most of all, her love for others is what gets her through it all. She is one of the most giving, kind souls I have ever met and her positive energy, her words and her gifts that she gives each day is precisely what the world needs."
~Debbie O.

"Joy Mills is a consummate professional in her field. Upon meeting her, she is reserved, courteous, and will weigh her words carefully with you. After you've been read a couple of times, and she learns your personality, she will give you a pack for your punch! She is a tender but tough soul, who has been through a lot in her life, thereby understanding how much her clients need from her at their readings. I'm glad I was referred to her as a client over ten years ago, as she was an immense source of help to me with learning to walk through my husband's suicide. I'm proud to now be able to call her my friend."
~Maria B.

"The day I met Joy Mills, it changed my life forever. I still recall when our paths crossed in 2006, as if it were yesterday. I was astonished by her gift of clairvoyance, her passion to help people, and her dedication to guide me down life's journey. Our paths have continued to cross over the years, and she truly has been given a fabulous gift from the Universe. I have been blessed to work with Joy on a regular basis. She never tells you what you want to hear, but will always tell you what you need to hear. I have received phenomenal advice from her that has helped me in both my life and career. Whether seeing her for a psychic session, reading one of her books, or having a drink with her over some laughs, she is always at her best. There is no doubt that

Joy has left a fingerprint on my life that will never be erased…. Anyone that crosses Joy's path has been given a great gift from the Universe! I am truly blessed to call her my friend."
~Laurie C

"Joy Mills has the gift of pure insight! Unparalleled to any other I have seen or witnessed. Joy shares her gift, much like herself, with wisdom, Love, knowledge and great authenticity. My personal readings with Joy, like the truth, have been scary real, cathartic, loving, insightful, tough and uplifting. I am grateful for Joy and her gift."
~Cate M.

"There are a few people one meets along their journey that can be trusted to help guide them through the wormholes of life's biggest moments. Joy is one of those people. Firmly connected to a universal kindness and love, Joy has always met her own craggy life moments head-on and helped me do the same. Having walked through an intense and rapid-fire period of grief recently (Mother, Sister, Father and Beloved Dog). I have learned just how valuable it is to have a friend and mentor like Joy.

Pain of loss, especially of a parent/Mother, who walked through life damaged herself, brought up a kaleidoscope of feelings for me. Some days truly were diamonds and some days were surly stones. Walking through these times was made easier with the help of Joy's wisdom, calm understanding and practical advice. It has always been Joy's purpose to be of service to all she meets. She shines on for many of us, helping to lead our way out of pain and into love and growth."
~Ann F

# About the Author

Joy M. Mills is an internationally known clairvoyant who has written, lectured and taught over many years. She has done numerous television appearances, radio and magazine articles. Joy is a published author, whose books and CDs are sold throughout the world in bookstores and online.

Joy resides with her husband and family in the St. Louis area where she teaches and maintains a private practice.